A
GREAT
CLOUD *of*
WITNESSES

A GREAT CLOUD *of* WITNESSES

A STUDY OF THOSE WHO LIVED BY FAITH

TRILLIA J. NEWBELL

MOODY PUBLISHERS
CHICAGO

Edited by Amanda Cleary Eastep
Interior and cover design: Erik M. Peterson
Cover illustration of mountains copyright © 2017 by Elinalee / iStock (684450764). All rights reserved.
Author photo: Lillian Prince Photography

Published in association with Don Gates, THE GATES GROUP @ www.the-gates-group.com.

All websites and phone numbers listed herein are accurate at the time of publication but may change in the future or cease to exist. The listing of website references and resources does not imply publisher endorsement of the site's entire contents. Groups and organizations are listed for informational purposes, and listing does not imply publisher endorsement of their activities.

Library of Congress Cataloging-in-Publication Data

Names: Newbell, Trillia J., author.
Title: A great cloud of witnesses : a study of those who lived by faith / Trillia Newbell.
Description: Chicago : Moody Publishers, [2021] | Includes bibliographical references. | Summary: "Enter the stories of the faithful in A Great Cloud of Witnesses. This six-week Bible study dives into Hebrews 11, examining the lives of Rahab, Enoch, Gideon, Sarah, and many more whose faiths withstood the tests of their days. By studying the great cloud of witnesses, your own faith will be strengthened to run the race before you"-- Provided by publisher.
Identifiers: LCCN 2020034995 (print) | LCCN 2020034996 (ebook) | ISBN 9780802421074 | ISBN 9780802499172 (ebook)
Subjects: LCSH: Bible. Hebrews, XI--Textbooks.
Classification: LCC BS2775.55 .N49 2021 (print) | LCC BS2775.55 (ebook) | DDC 227/.870071--dc23
LC record available at https://lccn.loc.gov/2020034995
LC ebook record available at https://lccn.loc.gov/2020034996

Originally delivered by fleets of horse-drawn wagons, the affordable paperbacks from D. L. Moody's publishing house resourced the church and served everyday people. Now, after more than 125 years of publishing and ministry, Moody Publishers' mission remains the same—even if our delivery systems have changed a bit. For more information on other books (and resources) created from a biblical perspective, go to www.moodypublishers.com or write to:

Moody Publishers
820 N. LaSalle Boulevard
Chicago, IL 60610

1 3 5 7 9 10 8 6 4 2

Printed in the United States of America

To my dearest son, Weston.

May the Lord grant you faith that leads to trust that leads
to obedience that leads to action.

May you forever rest in Him as you grow up, bearing fruit
in every good work.

CONTENTS

About This Study *9*

Introduction *19*

Week One: Once for All *22*

Week Two: The Possibility of Faith *38*

Week Three: The Well-Known *56*

Week Four: A Faith That Points to Jesus *76*

Week Five: The Powerful and Faithful *94*

Week Six: The Beaten, Persecuted, and Martyred *112*

Conclusion: The Founder and Perfecter of Our Faith *130*

Resources for Further Study *135*

Appendix A: A Note to Bible Study Leaders *136*

Appendix B: Four Practical Guidelines for Reading Old Testament Stories *141*

ABOUT THIS STUDY

I haven't figured out whether it's acceptable or not to have a favorite book in the Bible. I mean, it's God's Word, and every word is a gift! But let's face it, there are books we tend to gravitate toward over and over again. The book of Hebrews is one for me and, more specifically, I draw great comfort from the lives of those featured in Hebrews 11 who have gone before me. These Old Testament saints are known as the "great cloud of witnesses," as referenced in Hebrews 12:1, and often called the "Hall of Faith." But before we dive into the study, I want to help you get the most out of our time together by highlighting some things you'll be doing over the next six or eight weeks. My prayer is that you will be inspired and encouraged as you read about the lives of those highlighted in the great cloud of witnesses.

* * *

I love books. I love reading books, collecting books that I hope to read, and, except for the occasional agony over words to say, writing books. When I read a book, I typically read it from beginning to end (okay, sometimes I don't finish my books!). I don't read one sentence here and one sentence there. I'll read the entire paragraph or chapter. I think most people read books that way. There's nothing unique or even earth-shattering about that statement. Yet, when it comes to Bible reading, we often approach the greatest book of all differently.

The Bible is a book with many authors, all inspired by the Holy Spirit (2 Tim. 3:16). The Bible is filled with narratives, poetry, letters, and history. The Bible should be read and studied. Maybe I don't have to convince you to study since you've picked up this Bible study! But what I'd like for you to be prepared to do is work. I don't want you to get into the first week and be surprised that part of studying the Bible is to read it.

We are going to be reading Old Testament passages and stories. It will take time to read further to fully understand the context of the text or passages. It will take time to cross-reference to understand how it fits into the narrative of the whole Bible. Studying God's Word isn't meant to be drudgery. It's exhilarating.

The late R. C. Sproul reflected on a conversation he had when he was hired to teach at a school. The school wanted someone young who could make the text come alive. He wrote:

> I had to force myself to swallow my words. I wanted to say, "You want me to make the Bible come alive? I didn't know that it had died. In fact, I never even heard that it was ill. Who was the attending physician at the Bible's demise?" No, I can't make the Bible come alive for anyone. The Bible is already alive. It makes me come alive.[1]

Yes! The Word is living and active. The Word makes us come alive. But the question we must ask ourselves is: are we willing to read it beyond the quick Bible fixes? I know you are. And I'm excited to join you in this journey. Bible study takes time, and doing this study means you will need to set aside time to read. I want you to come expecting the Lord to teach you something. The Bible is alive, and for so many of us, we've only tasted a minuscule portion of it because we don't read it.

So, there's no surprises. You now know that in order to get the most out of this study you will need to read. You are going to read to study. You are going to read to gain understanding. And you are going to read narrative stories to understand the context of the book of Hebrews. It's going to be wonderful . . . and it's going to be work.

WHAT THIS STUDY OFFERS

If you have used my study on Romans 8, *If God Is For Us*, you will be happy to know that the format is quite similar. The biggest difference is that we will spend much of our time in the Old Testament to learn about the life and stories of the members of the Hall of Faith featured in Hebrews 11. This study is not meant to spoon-feed you the answers, although I do try to guide you toward them. The goal is that you will dig into the text and let the questions be your guide.

---

1. R. C. Sproul, *Knowing Scripture* (Downers Grove, IL: InterVarsity, 1977), 15.

This six-week study is unique in that it is a hybrid—a Bible study and devotional. Each week will include the following:

- A brief introduction to the week's study.

- Weekly "Read" prompts to get you into the Word.

- "Respond" questions to help you dig into what you've read and understand it better. These are the core Bible study questions you'll work through each week.

- Five days' worth of "Explore" devotionals each week to support you in thinking about the text and applying it to your life.

- Five days' worth of "Reflect" questions to give you more to think and pray about.

This study is also unique because of who I've chosen to focus our attention on. We will not study every Old Testament person named in Hebrews 11. I have decided to give greater attention to little-known or studied people, such as Enoch, Rahab, and Gideon. Toward the end of the study, we will also look at a few modern-day martyrs and spend time in prayer.

MAKE IT WORK FOR YOU!

I encourage you to take advantage of the flexibility built into this study to make it work for you. It's designed to be done in a group setting or individually. Here are a few of the possibilities.

- Do the study entirely on your own at home.

- Meet daily with a few friends in person (maybe for coffee) or online to share your response to the devotionals and the questions.

- Gather with a larger group through Bible studies offered at your church.

- Try a combination—do some of it (like the devotionals) at home and some of it (like selected study or reflection questions) in a weekly group gathering. Or study at home and then come together to discuss your insights and discoveries.

You can follow the suggested pattern of five days of study, two days off, or you can stretch out the material to cover six or even seven days. Personally, I like the idea of reading and study on one day, devotionals and reflections on five more days, and then taking a "sabbath" day of rest.

SIX- OR EIGHT-WEEK OPTIONS

This study also provides the flexibility to complete it in six or eight weeks! Within the study are two natural breaks that allow for extending the timeline to eight weeks. The first is in "Week One: Assurance of Things Hoped For." In the Respond section, simply stop at question 7, then begin week two with question 8. The second place is the conclusion at the end of the study. The conclusion, focused on Hebrews 12:1–3, is meant to be read as a devotional and applied, but can also stand alone as the study for week eight.

SIX WEEKS

Week One: Once for All

Week Two: The Possibility of Faith

Week Three: The Well-Known

Week Four: A Faith That Points to Jesus

Week Five: The Powerful and Faithful

Week Six: The Beaten, Persecuted, and Martyred

Conclusion: The Founder and Perfecter of Our Faith

EIGHT WEEKS

Week One: Once for All (ending with Respond question #7)

Week Two: Once for All continued (beginning with Respond question #8)

Week Three: The Possibility of Faith

Week Four: The Well-Known

Week Five: A Faith That Points to Jesus

Week Six: The Powerful and Faithful

Week Seven: The Beaten, Persecuted, and Martyred

Week Eight (Conclusion): The Founder and Perfecter of Our Faith

STUDYING THE BIBLE

Don't skip this section!

The temptation for all of us is to jump right in and begin studying. But I want you to read this section first, whether you are new to studying the Bible or a "seasoned pro." It never hurts for us to refresh our understanding for reading the text. Also, I have important notes sprinkled throughout that will help you read Hebrews 11. (These steps apply to studying any part of the Bible. But at the end of the study, I share an appendix to assist you in reading Old Testament stories.)

Step #1: Read the Passage Straight Through in One Sitting

The Bible is the inspired Word of God (1 Cor. 2:12–13; 2 Tim. 3:16–17), but it is also a book! Therefore, I encourage you to begin your study of any part of the Bible by simply reading it that way—like a book. Feel free to write down certain themes you see, repeated words, and key terms, but don't get bogged down in the details at first.

For the purposes of this study, in fact, I suggest that you begin by reading the entire book of Hebrews straight through. This will give you a sweeping overview and provide a helpful perspective when we get to Hebrews 11. Also, to help us study the faithful and understand the new covenant, we will begin our study in Hebrews 10.

Note also that although this is a New Testament study, we will be in the Old Testament throughout much of our study. While you read about the life of the Old Testament saints, jot down notes and various details of the story. Remember that God is the hero of each story. Look for how God intervened, sustained, showed Himself faithful, etc. Take a moment to gain a general understanding of the context: what was going on around the time of the story? For example, we will be studying Rahab. To find the context you might ask: why were the spies in Jericho?

Step #2: Clarify the Context

Have you ever walked up to some friends talking or overheard a conversation that seemed off or even inappropriate? I have. Once I walked up on a conversation and heard a woman say she had thrown a cat out of a window. I was confused and upset.

But I quickly discovered that in context, her statement made sense. She had thrown a stuffed toy out of a window and down to a little girl. Knowing the context of that conversation helped me a lot—and clarifying context helps us understand Scripture as well. We often go straight to the application without fully understanding the text itself.

What kind of context are we looking for when it comes to Bible study? For any book or passage, we need to consider:

- Who wrote it?

- When was it written?

- Who was it written for (the audience)?

- Why was it written (its purpose)?

- What was going on with God's people and the world in general when it was written?

- How does it relate to other parts of God's Word?

If you don't know the answers to any of these context questions, the section below will show you good places to look for help.

Step #3: Consider What the Passage Says—and What It Means

Once you have done those early steps, it's time to look for the meaning.

Often the meaning is clear, but sometimes you may need to reread, ponder, and maybe even look up the words before you have a clear sense of what it is saying. (Many of the "Respond" questions in this book are designed to help you do just that.)

This is a great time for cross-referencing. Cross-referencing—as the name implies—simply means comparing the passage you are studying to other passages in the Bible that can help you understand the meaning of the text. Looking at the text surrounding the verse you are reading also helps with both context and interpretation.

I always find it helpful to look for the gospel in the text—how it relates to Jesus and His saving work in the world. Since the whole of God's story points to Jesus, you can do this even with Old Testament texts, which we will see in this study.

Step #4: Apply the Text to Your Life

The Bible's message is meant to be lived as well as read, so look closely for what God is telling you through His Word. Sometimes the application will practically leap out on the page. Other times, you might have to live with the text, reflect on it, and pray about it. That's okay. The more time you spend in the Word, relying on the Holy Spirit, the more you'll find yourself turning to it for guidance.

I would like to give one clarification about applying the circumstances and responses of people featured in the Old Testament to your life. As we seek to apply, in the context of Hebrews 11, we are looking for ways to imitate the Old Testament characters' faith. These are narrative in nature (stories that really happened); and therefore, we want to approach them like we would a fictional story, looking for the plot, climax, characters, events, theme, etc. In finding those things, we learn.

Our approach is similar. For example, we are not attempting to obey God as He directed Abraham to leave everything and head to a foreign land. We are, however, desirous of imitating the faith it took for Abraham to get up and go. And perhaps, in application, you could apply that to your own journey, but God is not necessarily commanding that you go to a foreign land.[2]

To sum it up, here's what you will do:

1. Read the passage

2. Clarify the context

3. Answer: What does the passage say and mean?

4. Apply it to your life

Need help?

As you read through the book of Hebrews and attempt to answer the questions in this study, you may find yourself struggling at times, especially if you are new to Hebrews and to Bible study in general. The writer of Hebrews addresses topics such as old and new covenant, priesthood, the sacrificial system, warnings against apostasy, and exhortations. It is a rich and deeply encouraging letter about the greatness of Jesus.

---

2. Dr. Jason Hood has a helpful article about applying Hebrews 11 to your life. You can read it at https://www.thegospelcoalition.org/article/imitate-biblical-heroes/.

I believe without a doubt you should be able to pick up the Bible and read it without the aid of other resources. However, you might also discover you need a little more background or explanation about the author's references, the meaning of certain words, or how the concepts in Hebrews 11 compare to other parts of Hebrews or the Bible in general. Or you might simply want to dig deeper into the text, as many of the study questions in this book encourage you to do.

Where do you go for help? Start with your own Bible! Chances are it contains most of what you need to understand what you are reading. Many Bibles include a concordance or cross-references (to direct you to other places in the Bible where a particular idea can be found), background notes, and even commentaries.

If your Bible doesn't have these aids—or if you want more help—a wealth of other resources is readily available, and you don't have to spend a lot of money and time to make use of them. Here are a few possibilities:

Other versions of the Bible. I primarily use the English Standard Version (ESV), which gives a very accurate word-for-word translation of the authors' original Greek, and I have used this translation as a basis for this study. Many of the "Respond" questions refer directly to the wording of the ESV, so you may have an easier time with them if you also use it. But you may find some other versions helpful as a supplement, and of course the ESV is not a requirement. Two online sites that put different translations and paraphrases at your fingertips are biblegateway.com and biblehub.com.

Study aids. You don't have to buy a library of commentaries, Bible dictionaries, lexicons, and such to find some help. If your church has a library, look there. You can find excellent help at biblegateway.com, biblehub.com (my favorite!), and several other sites.

Other resources. In the footnotes, you'll see books, videos, articles, and other resources I've consulted while preparing this study. I recommend them for further exploration.

Other Christians! If you're doing this study with a group, you'll be able to compare notes with other members. But even if you're doing it on your own, seek out opportunities to ask questions or compare notes with others. You will benefit from unique perspectives.

However you choose to approach this study, I hope you will find it enriching and inspiring—six weeks or eight weeks that draw you closer to Christ and give you a deeper and more grateful appreciation for His Word and the gospel.

INTRODUCTION

The book of Hebrews is unique in its style and authorship. Let's start with authorship, which is unknown, as the writer does not identify himself in the text.[3] And although the book does not begin with a greeting as a typical letter does, the end of the epistle indicates that Hebrews was written as a letter (Heb. 13:19; 22–25). The writer is clearly familiar with his readers. And because the author mentions Timothy in these texts, we can deduce that it was written in the first century.

We also see from Hebrews 13:22 that the author labels his letter as an exhortation with all the elements of a long sermon. He desires his readers to endure in the faith, which I encourage you to explore as you read through Hebrews. Where do you see the theme of enduring in the faith and not leaving Jesus? Write it down as you read. He urges his readers to remain in the Lord and build up their faith by encouraging them to look to those who have gone before us (Heb. 11).

Finally, as we'll see in our study, the readers must have had a thorough knowledge of the Old Testament. The author refers to it throughout Hebrews, essentially pointing out that Jesus is better. Jesus is supreme over all systems and things, whether human or otherwise. Throughout we see the author comparing one thing or another to the greatness of Christ. We see in Hebrews 10 that these Christians must have needed this reminder because they were suffering. And we need these reminders, too.

Our entire Christian walk is a "walk by faith, not by sight" (2 Cor. 5:7). God has graciously made it clear to us that He knows this to be true, and, in His kindness, has given us examples in the Scriptures of those who have gone before us. Understanding faith, growing in it, and living by it are key elements to finishing our race (Heb. 12:1–2). Understanding the basis of our faith is of utmost importance. And setting our eyes on the object of our faith is the only way we'll endure.

Every day we are operating by faith, whether we realize it or not. Our faith is tested; our faith is stretched. Our faith can falter. Life is a fight for faith to believe and

---

3. Although we do not know the author and some have argued that it could have been Priscilla, for the sake of brevity and ease of reading, I will use male pronouns if "the writer" or "our author" is not possible.

trust God. Over the next several weeks, we will explore Hebrews 11 and many of the Old Testament passages and characters this chapter highlights so that our faith may be built and strengthened as we live out the Christian life.

Ultimately, we will learn to run back to our Savior in faith. Each week we will study the lives of flawed yet faithful servants who endured great suffering, obeyed the Lord, and, in some instances, were even killed for their faith. Scripture tells us to look at this "cloud of witnesses" (Heb. 12:1) and remember their stories as motivation to run the race set before us. Stories are powerful tools the Lord uses to inspire, challenge, and encourage us in the faith. My hope is that we will come away eager to stay the course, knowing those who went before us, as we fix our eyes on the One who sustains us and keeps us.

You can use this chart[4] as a quick guide and reference as you walk through Hebrews 11. This does not include the many unnamed saints that the author had in mind as noted in Hebrews 11:32–38.[5]

By Faith	Hebrews	Cross Reference
Abel	11:4	Genesis 4
Enoch	11:5	Genesis 5:18–24
Noah	11:7	Genesis 5:29–10:32
Abraham	11:8–19	Genesis 12–25
Sarah	11:11	Genesis 12–23
Isaac	11:17–20	Genesis 17–35
Jacob	11:21	Genesis 25–50
Joseph	11:21–22	Genesis 37–50
Moses	11:23–28	Exodus 2–3
Rahab	11:31	Joshua 2; 6:17–25
Gideon	11:32	Judges 6–8
Barak	11:32	Judges 4–5
Samson	11:32	Judges 13–16
Jephthah	11:32	Judges 11–12; 1 Samuel 12:11
David	11:32	1–2 Samuel
Samuel	11:32	1 Samuel

4. Adapted from the ESV® Study Bible (The Holy Bible, English Standard Version®), copyright ©2008 by Crossway, a publishing ministry of Good News Publishers. Used by permission. All rights reserved.

5. As mentioned throughout the study, the devotionals, which dive into the narratives and applying them to our lives, will not cover every person named in this list. However, the main Bible study questions each week labeled "Respond" will take you through each character. This chart was inspired by The Hall of Faith in Hebrews 11 chart in the ESV Study Bible. ESV Study Bible, ed. Wayne Grudem (Wheaton, IL: Crossway, 2008), 2382. The Scriptures referenced do not necessarily cover the entire life of the biblical character.

Now if you have time before digging into the first week's homework, take some time to read the whole book of Hebrews.

Once for All

Although most of our time will be spent in the Old Testament, we will set up the study with a strong understanding of the intent of the author of Hebrews, and a definition of faith. We find much of that starting in Hebrews 10. There, we find the greatness of Christ—His one and done, all-satisfying sacrifice for all who would believe, securing our redemption and abolishing the need for rituals. We see the comparison of the supremacy of Christ to all other things clearly in this chapter as well: The new covenant, ushered in by Jesus, is better than the old covenant, and Jesus is better than Mosaic animal sacrifices.

We can be sure of all that God has done through His Son—we can draw near; we can hold on to our faith as we wait for our Savior to return. And we can entrust ourselves to the living God. Hebrews 10 sets us up for learning about the faithful so that we might emulate their faith. In many ways, we see the why before we see the how. In this chapter, we begin to understand why you and I can walk by faith.

READ | **HEBREWS 10**

RESPOND

These are the core Bible study questions you'll work through this week:

1. The chapter opens with a mention of the law. What is the law the writer is referring to? Although the reference is clearly in the Old Testament, the book of Hebrews provides glimpses of the law's covenants, sacrifices, and priesthood.

2. What does it mean by "a shadow"?

3. Hebrews uses the words "draw near" in several places. What is the significance of drawing near? How does one draw near according to 10:1–3?

4. A sacrifice is a sacrifice, right? Not according to Hebrews. Why can't the blood of bulls and goats (Levitical sacrifices) take away sins once and for all? (See verses 3–10.)

5.   In verses 11–14 the writer summarizes the previous text. "Perfected for all time" does not mean that you and I are sinless; what does it mean that "he has perfected for all time those who are being sanctified" (v. 14)?

6.   Verses 15–18 are cited from Hebrews 8:10; Hebrews 8:10 is cited from Jeremiah 31:31–34. What is the significance of this text in Jeremiah?

7.   "New covenant" is the focus of Jeremiah 31:31–34. What does the text mean by "new covenant"? (A quick search reveals that this mention of new covenant is the only one found in the Old Testament.)

There will be two places—one this week and one at the end of the study—where you will be able to extend your study to eight weeks. Pause after question 7 if you are doing an eight-week study. Pick up on question 8 next week. If you do end on question 7 the first week of your study, go ahead and answer these questions to complete Week One of the core Bible study questions:

Where is Jesus in these verses? Where do you see the gospel? What do you learn about God and His character in these verses? How might you apply theses verses to your life?

Pick up on question 8 for the second week. Otherwise, continue this week with question 8.

8.   "Therefore" means that the texts, chapters, or a significant point before these verses explains the why in v. 19. Why can "we have confidence to enter the holy places"? What are the holy places? (Other versions of the Bible use "Most Holy Place.")

9.   If the verses before the "therefore" share the *why*, the rest of verses 19–22 share the *how*. Can you list how we are able to enter the holy place?

10. The writer begins to share three exhortations in verses 19–25 (draw near, hold fast, consider). An exhortation is one way the biblical writers urge the hearers or readers toward something. In each case, what is he urging us to do? How and why?

11. In verse 26, the writer goes from exhortation to warning about the judgment of God. The writer is not warning against sinning in general. In these verses, he is warning against apostasy, or renouncing the faith, which can only happen if one knows the truth and then chooses to reject it.

12. What do you think it means to "set aside the law of Moses" (v. 28)? What was the punishment for the outright rejection of the law? The writer contrasts this Old Testament punishment with rejecting Jesus (v. 29). Why was this punishment worse? And what is this judgment (vv. 29–31)?

13. Again, our author takes a sharp turn from exhortation, warning, and now reassurance. The writer asks his readers to remember how they persevered through suffering. Why did they endure joyfully? What is the "better possession" (vv. 32–35)?

14. According to Hebrews 10:37–39 and Habakkuk 2:3–4, which is the text quoted, what happens when we shrink back (or what do we need to remember so that we *don't* shrink back)? What does it mean to shrink back?

15. Where is Jesus in these verses? Where do you see the gospel?

16. What do you learn about God and His character in these verses?

17. How might you apply theses verses to your life?

WEEK ONE | DAY ONE

EXPLORE

Sin's Daily Reminder, God's Ultimate Sacrifice

READ | HEBREWS 10:1–14

Have you ever watched a dog find its shadow? It's delightful and often hilarious. Dogs will bark at the shadow as if seeing another dog. There's something so curious about a shadow. Kids play with their shadows, discovering ways to change their shape and appearance—a little bit longer here, a little shorter there. There's something about a shadow that is similar, but altogether different than the original source. For example, a shadow is not the same as the dog. A shadow can't do what a dog can do.

Similarly, we see the author refers to the law as a shadow (10:1). Specifically, the text is referring to the laws pertaining to priesthood, covenant, and sacrifices (see Heb. 7:11–9:29). So, we have a picture of a shadow, something that can only tell of or foreshadow the good things to come.

Every year priests would sacrifice an animal as a reminder of their sin and their need for a savior. God's ultimate sacrifice did away with the practice of sacrifices— we no longer must sacrifice anything to receive full forgiveness. Our sacrifices can never take away sin. Sometimes we try and try, thinking our efforts will save us. Only God's finished work can take away sin. And He accomplished it through the "good thing" that has come—the perfect and finished work of Jesus (Heb. 10:1).

REFLECT

1. What do you think it would be like if we had to sacrifice an animal each year?

2. Do you ever struggle with trusting that the sacrifice of Jesus is enough? If so, how?

3. How do you fight the temptation to think you must offer something to the Lord to be forgiven?

4. What is the difference between denying ourselves and the sacrificing that we are discussing in this text?

WEEK ONE | DAY TWO

EXPLORE

Draw Near with a True Heart and Full Assurance

READ | HEBREWS 10:15–22

In my work, I have the opportunity to speak with people I may never see again in this life. I go to a location, share God's Word, and then I head home. I've often found that in those contexts, people are extremely open with me. I wonder if it's because they know that I won't see them again, so they feel a sort of freedom to share. Or maybe it's because I'm not all that threatening (at 5′2″). Recently, I had one such interaction. A college student thanked me for my talk and then shared that she lacked assurance of her faith and didn't think she could draw near to the Lord. As we talked, I gathered that she lacked confidence because she was comparing herself to others, focusing on how she felt, and worrying she wasn't doing enough.

I imagine many of us wouldn't feel confident to draw near to the Lord if we spent enough time focusing on those things. We all fall short. If our goodness was the measure for when and how we approach God, well, I don't think I'd ever do it!

But that's the good news for all of us. In these texts, we see why we can draw near. Our confidence doesn't come from our abilities. Our confidence is in the blood of Jesus (10:14). He opened the way to the Father. And because of this truth, we can draw near with a true heart—believing that what Jesus has done is enough. Our confidence, assurance, and trust aren't in our flesh, they're in Him.

Today, if you have placed your faith and trust in the finished work of Jesus, look to Him as you go to Him. Our assurance comes from Jesus—He who promised is faithful (10:23).

REFLECT

1. What often keeps you from running to Jesus?

2. Have you ever struggled with doubt in your salvation? Do you now? Find a faithful friend to share about Jesus and encourage your faith.

3. What are other Scriptures that remind us that we can draw near to God because of Jesus?

4. We can rest in knowing that Christ will hold us fast (Rom. 8:31–39; Phil. 3:12; Jude 24), so why do you believe we are exhorted to "hold fast the confession of our hope" (Heb. 10:23)?

WEEK ONE | DAY THREE

EXPLORE

Building Each Other Up

READ | **HEBREWS 10:24-25**

As I type, the world is in the middle of a terrible pandemic. Everything is shut down. It will be a time that may irrevocably change how we interact and will undoubtedly be studied and written about for years to come. It's also an unprecedented time in the history of the church. Almost no church on the planet is gathering for worship—in person. For the safety of our neighbors and due to the government's recommendations, people are not allowed to gather in groups and must remain six feet apart.

As I come to this text here in Hebrews, it carries a greater weight than perhaps it did before. The writer sticks this admonishment in the middle of theological teaching about the person of Jesus and what He has accomplished on the cross. Therefore, it is of utmost importance that we pay attention. We need others to help us faithfully hold fast our confession without wavering. We need others to endure in the Christian life. And you and I have the privilege to stir up—encourage—those around us.

It can be easy in times of prosperity or peace to forget our need for one another. But as we see here, it's not a matter of season. We are urged to build each other up "all the more as [we] see the Day drawing near." We don't know the time or day of Jesus' return, but we know He is coming. It is on that day that every knee will bow and every tongue confess that Jesus is Lord (Rom. 14:11; Phil. 2:10–11).

One of the miracles of the period of the pandemic has been watching the unique ways the church has been able to connect with one another. In the technology age, most of us are without excuse—we can still connect one way or another. Today, you and I have the privilege to encourage one another. Let's take every opportunity.

REFLECT

1. Have you ever experienced a season when you struggled to see the value of gathering with other Christians? Do you now?

2. Why do you think it's important to "stir up one another up to love and good works"?

3. Where are other places in the Scriptures where we see the value of Christian fellowship?

4. What do you think is the significance of the writer drawing attention to the coming day of Christ's return and judgment? Do you see that urgency in other places in Scripture?

WEEK ONE | DAY FOUR

Putting Off Sin

READ | HEBREWS 10:26–31

In the previous devotional, we see that there is an urgency for Christians to meet together and encourage one another. That urgency is because the day the Lord returns is drawing near (vv. 24–25). No one knows the time or day of the Lord's return except for the Father (Matt. 24:36). The point is that we live as those expecting to see our Savior—we live anticipating that the day will indeed come.

As we come to verse 26 in Hebrews 10, we see that part of the response to the truth of Christ's return is that we no longer continue in sin.

It's important to note that the author is writing to those who have heard the truth. The person who has heard the truth of the gospel and believes knows all that Jesus has done on her behalf. She understands and yet she continues to deliberately sin. It's a willful sinning. The author does us a service to warn us that God will judge His people (Heb. 10:30). The author is addressing someone who has completely deserted Jesus and the truth of God's Word. He is warning against apostasy (Heb. 6:4–6).

The older I get, the more dear friends I've watched decide to no longer follow Jesus. It is heartbreaking to watch people walk away from the faith. Some leave due to hurt. Others leave because the world and the desires of the flesh are too enticing to refuse. I do not fear this for myself. I believe wholeheartedly in the promise that God will finish the good work He began in us (Phil. 1:6).[6] But I also do not believe I am strong enough in and of myself not to fall (1 Cor. 10:12).

Cling to Jesus. Abide—draw close to—Him. He is a keeping God. We have the honor of knowing Him. When you and I sin, we can confess it to the Lord who forgives us and will change us. Deliberate sin is unrepentant, continuing sin. You and I can instead put off sin and receive God's grace.

REFLECT

1. Why is repentance important if we have Jesus?

2. Have you ever been in a season when you realized you were "sinning deliberately"? What led you to confess and pursue restoration?

3. If not you, have you ever seen a friend go through this time and be restored? How did that encourage you in the faith?

4. How does knowing and understanding truth help us continue in the faith?

---

6. Theologians are torn about apostasy and whether or not those who are Christians, true Christians, can actually leave the faith or "fall away." For further study, I wrote about this debate in *Sacred Endurance*. Trillia J. Newbell, *Sacred Endurance: Finding Grace and Strength for a Lasting Faith* (Downers Grove, IL: IVP, 2019), 173–78.

WEEK ONE | DAY FIVE

Suffering and Faith to Endure

READ | HEBREWS 10:32–39

Suffering has a way of bringing you to your knees before the Lord. We all mourn differently but one thing I consistently see is people asking for prayer. There's something innate in us, whether we know God truly or not, that knows that God exists and only He can handle our circumstances. And for Christians, we can testify that He not only knew about it, He was faithful to us through it.

After warnings and exhortations, the writer reminds his listeners to remember their previous suffering. There's something about remembering how the Lord preserved you through something in the past that can build and renew faith for today. Those who suffered in this context of Hebrews, experienced public reproach (most likely imprisonment for their faith; see Heb. 13:3) and afflictions we may never experience. They were likely persecuted for their faith. But during their suffering, they extended compassion and welcomed their property being destroyed because they had their eyes fixed on a better position—an eternal one (v. 34). Because of this, the writer urges them not to throw away their confidence. The Lord is still with them.

I think we all need to be reminded to remember our past trials when facing new ones. Because of the hope that we have, we can continue in the faith and endure the trials ahead of us. We need patience to persevere. The Lord may come slowly (at least in our estimation), but we know He is coming. So, we live by faith as we wait; not shrinking back but enduring in faith.

REFLECT

1. Do you remember a time you endured a hard trial? What are some ways you experienced the Lord's faithfulness?

2. How did you respond to that trial and what did you learn?

3. Endurance is a theme in the Bible. Why do you think you have "need for endurance"?

4. The writer quotes Habakkuk 2:3–4, and then declares we are not ones who shrink back. What might it look like to shrink back?

The Possibility of Faith

Hebrews 11:1–3 will be our guide into the Great Cloud of Witnesses. Those Old Testament saints died being sure of the things that were promised and entrusted themselves to the omniscient, omnipotent, eternal, faithful, and trustworthy God. God, in His goodness, honored their faith. We will learn what it means to have faith, establishing a working definition and understanding the nature of faith in the believer.

But it's important that we define faith. We will look at the text in hopes of coming to a clear conclusion, but here are a few ways that others define the faith that is described here in our text.

New Testament scholar Philip Hughes argued the limitations of using Hebrews 11:1–3 to define faith:

It is necessary to appreciate the limits of this definition of faith, for it is not exhaustive, and in particular it is placed within the perspective of hope, which in turn is aroused by divine promises—promises as yet unfulfilled in the experience of those men and women of faith who belonged to the age prior to the coming of Christ and whose heroic examples will illustrate our author's theme.[7]

Theologian F. F. Bruce has much to say about the meanings of words like *hypostasis* (confidence or assurance), which we explore below, but here's how he sums up the faith of Old Testament saints: "Their faith consisted simply in taking God at his word and directing their lives accordingly; things yet future as far as their experience went were thus present to faith, and things outwardly unseen were visible to the inward eye."[8]

And finally, pastor Richard Phillips explains that there are many definitions because of the broad meaning of the word *hypostasis*, which he leans heavily on Hughes to define. He believes that our author in Hebrews never intended us to establish a clear or narrow definition of the faith. He writes,

It seems that the writer of Hebrews deliberately chose a word that has a broad and rich array of meanings, all of which are to the point. Faith is the substance of things hoped for, it is the foundation upon which they are brought into being, it is a confident attitude toward those things God has promised, and faith is the guarantee that gives us a sure possession even now.[9]

7. Philip Edgcumbe Hughes, *A Commentary on the Epistle to the Hebrews* (Grand Rapids, MI: Eerdmans, 1977), 438.
8. F. F. Bruce, *The Epistle to the Hebrews* (Grand Rapids, MI: Eerdmans, 1990), 276.
9. Richard D. Philips, *Faith Victorious: Finding Strength and Hope from Hebrews 11* (Phillipsburg, NJ: P&R Publishing, 2002), 6.

And to all of these I say *yes* and *amen*! What does this mean for our purposes? You will read the text and determine a working definition for what it means that each saint walked "by faith." That working definition will guide you as you read their stories. There is hardly the chance of a wrong answer if you stay close to the text. And by all appearances, there are many answers that could fit well into this chapter.

But just as the writer goes straight to it, so will we. We will begin this week exploring the Old Testament stories that make up this great chapter. The writer begins at the beginning—before the flood (or antediluvian). The brotherly affection ran dry quickly for Cain and Abel, the sons of Adam and Eve. Theirs is a difficult story of envy, rage, and redemption as we learn about a faith that still speaks.

Next on the list is Enoch. Enoch is a mystery. He was mentioned as part of the genealogy in Genesis 5, but we have little information about his life. What we do know is that he walked closely with God. Enoch teaches us to walk closely and faithfully with our God, too. We spend a considerable amount of time exploring what we might glean from Enoch's brief mention in Scripture.

READ | HEBREWS 11:1–7; GENESIS 4:1–16; 5:21–24

RESPOND

These are the core Bible study questions you'll work through this week:

1. Define "assurance" (Greek, *hypostasis*). What are the things hoped for? Define conviction. What are the things not seen? This is your working definition for faith (Heb. 11:1).

2. For by [your answer in question 1] the people of old receive their _____. What is commendation (Heb. 11:2)?

3. Where else in Scripture do we see references like Hebrews 11:3; specifically, "the word of God" and "things that are visible"?

4. What did Abel do "by faith" (Heb. 11:4)?

5. The Scriptures compare the gifts of Cain vs. Abel. Why was Cain's gift not acceptable (Gen. 4:4, 7)?

6. How does Abel's faith still speak?

7. Who was Enoch, and what is he commended for (Gen. 5:21–24)?

8. What is the correlation or significance of faith and pleasing God (Heb. 11:5–6)?

9. "Draw near" (v. 6) can be found throughout the book of Hebrews. Where else have you seen it? What is the significance of drawing near?

10. Where is Jesus in these verses? Where do you see the gospel?

11. What do you learn about God and His character in these verses?

12. How might you apply theses verses to your life?

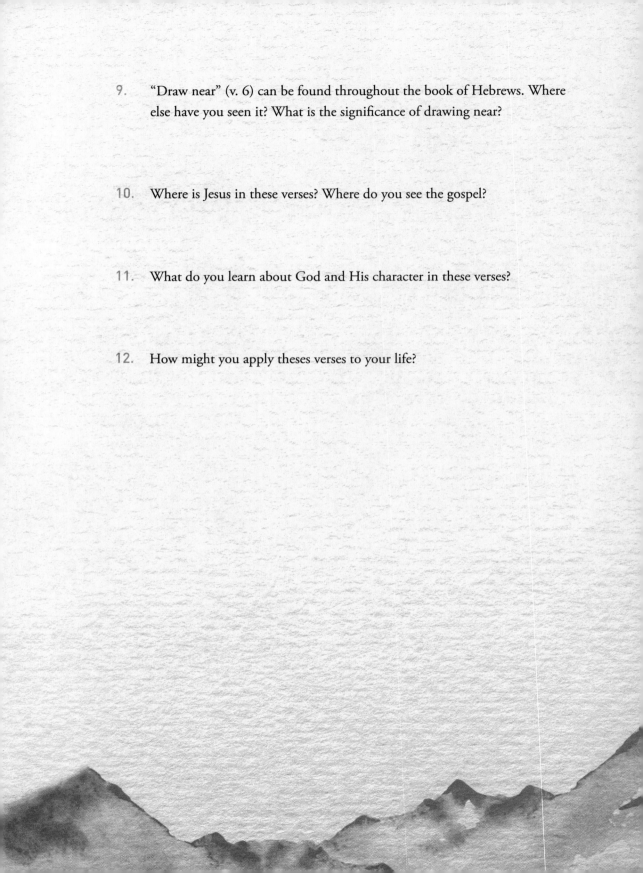

WEEK TWO | DAY ONE

Defining Faith

READ | HEBREWS 11:1–3

There's not much that I'm sure of. I don't know what my children will be when they grow up. I can't tell you how long I'll get to enjoy this time with my husband. I assume I know where I'll live over the next five years, but that could change. I don't even know what I'll be cooking next week! There's a great deal of unknowns in this life. Maybe that's why faith is called a gift in Ephesians 2:8–10.

In the context of Ephesians, faith is a gift because you and I can't earn our salvation—God grants faith to us. It is a free gift of God's grace. But I also believe faith is a gift because it's something that gives assurance and if you are assured of something you are confident. Faith is confidence in our hope. And our hope is in the promises of God. It is sure—a firm foundation.

It's important for us to understand this faith in the promises of God because none of the Old Testament characters we are about to study would have seen even what we have seen! These men and women had a conviction in the things not seen, and think about it: none of them had even experienced the birth, life, death, and resurrection of Jesus. These are all things that you and I know about—they have come to pass.

Faith then isn't something that's abstract or fluffy. Faith is a grounded assurance and conviction in the Lord and His Word, and it rests in all of His promises for today, tomorrow, and forevermore. We are all waiting for the second coming of Jesus—a thing not yet seen. We are all waiting for all things to be made new. So we ask God for continued faith to believe.

REFLECT

1.   How would you define faith in one sentence? What about one word?

2.   Why do you think the writer emphasizes things not seen?

3.   How might thinking about the creation account in Genesis build our faith to believe?

4.   What are practical ways you fight for faith?

WEEK TWO | DAY TWO

EXPLORE

A Faith that Still Speaks

READ | HEBREWS 11:4; GENESIS 4

Cain, the oldest son of Adam and Eve, worked on the land (farmer) and his younger brother, Abel, worked with sheep (herdsman). Cain offered the Lord fruit while Abel offered the Lord the firstborn of his flock (Gen. 4:3–4). The Lord wasn't pleased by Cain's offering because, as some scholars note, it wasn't a sacrificial offering.[10] He offered the leftovers rather than the first fruits. Abel's offering, however, was a sign of his faith—it was sacrificial.

Reading the account of Cain and Abel, I feel like I'm watching a movie, yelling at the screen, "Don't do it!" Right here we see that Cain gets angry, but the Lord gives Him a way of escape. The Lord informs Cain that sin is right there with him but that he can rule over it. Cain could have repented from his anger and moved on. Boy, I relate. I can't help but think of all the times I've allowed my sin to have its full effect on me. But by the grace of God, I've also experienced countless moments when the Lord reminded me that He has given me, too, a way of escape (1 Cor. 10:13). In the end, Cain kills his brother (Gen. 4:8).

Abel lived a short life—one that, looking on from a distance, would seem too tragic for anything good to come of it. He was the first person murdered in the Old Testament, and he died a senseless death at the hands of his own flesh and blood. But in his short life, Abel leaves us a legacy of faith. His faithful sacrifice is

---

10. *ESV Study Bible*, ed. Wayne Grudem (Wheaton, IL: Crossway, 2008), 57.

written for us to remember; his faith still speaks to us today. And it is noted that God counted Abel as righteous because of his faith (Heb. 11:4).

Thankfully, you and I do not have to present the Lord with an animal for our faith to be counted as righteous. But it wasn't as much the animal—remember, Cain presented something as well—as it was the heart of Abel. You and I can ask the Lord to give us a heart that worships Him, trusts in Him, and believes that He will provide as Abel did. His faith still speaks because it provides an example of faith lived out—even if for only a minute.

Most of us will only be remembered by our immediate family—our faith won't likely be written in a book that lasts centuries. But you and I can still leave a legacy of faith. My hope and prayer for each of us is that our faith outlasts us for generations to come. May our faith still speak, even if only to our immediate family.

REFLECT

1. You might have experienced a time when, like Cain, you gave in to the anger in your heart. What are ways that you fight the temptation to respond in anger?

2. Although God did punish Cain, He was merciful to him. If you read the account, you see that God would not allow anyone to kill him (Gen. 4:12–16). How have you seen the mercy of God in your life or the life of others?

3.   What are ways you can put your faith into action as Abel did?

4.   What are ways that you, regardless of marital status, children, etc., can leave a legacy of faith?

WEEK TWO | DAY THREE

Please note that we are going to spend more time with Enoch because he is a lesser-known person in the Word and he, too, has a faith that still speaks.

EXPLORE

Walk with God

READ | HEBREWS 11:5; GENESIS 5:21–24

The account of Enoch fascinates me. First, he walked with God and never died; God took Him! He was taken by God at the age of 365, but he fathered Methuselah who lived for 969 years.[11] His account in Genesis is extremely short but, as we see in Hebrews, it was incredibly important. His faithfulness should be emulated, so let's take a deeper look specifically at what it means to walk with God.

Enoch is noted to have walked with God, but God doesn't spell out what he did or how he did it. All we know is that Enoch's faith pleased the Lord (Gen. 5:22; Heb. 11:5–6). We know that to walk with God would mean a deep and abiding relationship. But the prophet Micah gives us a glimpse of what it might have meant for Enoch to walk with God. After the people of Israel ask questions about what they should bring to the Lord, what is required of them by God—all of which is outward focused rather than regarding the state of their hearts—God answered and the people responded: "He has told you, O man, what is good; and what does the LORD require of you but to do justice, and to love kindness, and to walk humbly with your God?" (Mic. 6:8).

---

11. See Genesis 5:21–27.

Jesus emphasized the importance of this aspect of faithfulness too. The Pharisees were sacrificing through their tithes but neglecting these weightier aspects of walking with God. Jesus said, "For you tithe mint and dill and cumin, and have neglected the weightier matters of the law: justice and mercy and faithfulness" (Matt. 23:23). Again we see the importance of justice, kindness, and faithfulness or humble walking, which is evidence of a transformed heart. So, it's a safe assumption based on the whole of Scripture to assume that Enoch walked in such a way.

And we can too. By God's grace, we can walk with an understanding of right and wrong (just living) and act in a way that loves our neighbor. As an extension of that, we can extend the same mercy to others as God has extended to us (loving kindness). And finally we can, by His grace, walk in a manner that acknowledges God as the Creator and ruler of the world (humbly). We can confess dependence on Him. And if we want to do justice and love mercy, we will need God.

To walk with God could simply be summed up as to enjoy a relationship with Him. It's in this relationship with God that we see the outward doing. It's an outward response to the ongoing relationship with the Lord that we all long to have. And at the end of our days, we too hope to be ones who are remembered to have walked with God.

REFLECT

1. Why do you think Enoch was included in Hebrews 11?

2.   When you consider what it means to "walk with God," what comes to mind?

3.   Why does the heart matter in relation to faith in action or what we do?

4.   What aspects or characteristics of the Lord help us walk humbly?

WEEK TWO | DAY FOUR

Faith in Obscurity: Enoch continued

READ | HEBREWS 11:5

When broadcasters highlight team sports, it's typical for them to shout out the standouts. So for football it might be the quarterback or an amazing running back. It's rare that announcers call out the holder for a field goal kicker. But you can't kick a successful field goal without someone holding the ball. When I think about Enoch's faith, I can't help but think about his obscurity, and yet God notices him. He notices the person who holds the ball for the field goal kicker, so to speak.

Enoch's account is short, but his faith is huge. His faith caught the attention of the Lord so much so that he is mentioned in Hebrews 11. But I imagine that most of us skimmed over him in our Bible reading. He is so obscure. It almost seems like a random inclusion. But God is not like man. God notices the faithfulness of Enoch. God notices his life—this little-known faithful saint.

As we continue through Hebrews 11, we see that the writer begins naming categories of people who were faithful (11:13–14, 29, 32–40). God doesn't put everyone's name in the Scriptures, but we can be certain that those He has counted as righteous, He will put in His book of life (Rev. 20:15). You and I will lead a life of faith mostly in obscurity. Enoch's account reminds us that faithful obedience—a life lived for the Lord—is not in vain. He would not have known that, hundreds of years after his death, he'd be remembered. But the writer of Hebrews reminds us: "For God is not unjust so as to overlook your work and the love that you have shown for his name in serving the saints, as you still do" (Heb. 6:10).

You and I don't need a stage, accolades, or acknowledgment. God isn't calling us to be noticed, He calls us to be faithful. And God in His goodness rewards that faithfulness—in the life to come. Keep going. He notices and that is all that matters. Enoch's faith is recorded in one line of Scripture, yet he is put in the Hall of Faith. His life was utterly important even though we don't know much about him. Faithfulness is what matters most.

REFLECT

1. Can you think of other important people in the Scriptures who are only mentioned once or twice?

2. Have you ever considered the work you do as unimportant? What truth from God's word encourages you during times of discouragement?

3. The world seems to value fame, and if we aren't careful, that desire can creep into our own hearts. What promises of reward in the Bible help you continue doing the work of ministry in your home, church, and community knowing that you may not receive any public acknowledgment for it?

4. Who in your local church or community do you think excels at faithful living in obscurity?

WEEK TWO | DAY FIVE

It's Possible to Please God

READ | **HEBREWS 11:6**

Margaret was hard to please. She was rarely satisfied. Her friends always felt like they were letting her down. Often, she would chastise them for things that weren't inherently wrong. And, boy, did she hold a grudge. If you crossed her, you were done for life . . . forever and always cast out of her inner circle, which was already quite small.

Obviously, Margaret is a fictional character, although I'm certain there are many "Margarets" out there. But I've also been Margaret before. I've held a grudge or have been easily irritated. Thankfully, during those times, I've repented and turned to receive God's grace.

But what if God was more like you and me? What if He was easily irritated? What if He held a grudge? Maybe you've heard this text quoted before, "Without faith it is impossible to please him" (Heb. 11:6). We typically quote this and think *great, then I can't and will never be able to please the Lord.* But this verse implies that it *is* possible to please God. And He rewards those who believe. Wow, it's pretty jaw-dropping amazing. God wants us to seek Him, draw near to Him, believe in Him, and what does He do? He rewards us.

If you do not believe in God—if you do not trust in His promises to you—then it doesn't please Him. If we draw near to the Lord, we ask the Lord to help us draw near with a true heart believing that Jesus intercedes for us and that God hears us. And if we don't believe, God tells us that we can tell Him and ask Him for faith to believe.

God is not like us. It pleases Him that we come to Him with our weak faith. You and I *get* to have a relationship with Him. It is to our benefit to know Him, and He's not hiding.

REFLECT

1. What are other Scriptures that help us remember that God is pleased with us, in spite of our sin?

2. Why do you think faith (believing in Him and His promises) pleases the Lord?

3. What is the measure of faith that you have used to approach the Lord? In other words, have you ever allowed how you feel to keep you from asking the Lord for help?

4. What are the rewards God has in store for those who believe?

The Well-Known

You may have heard their stories many times, but there's a good reason why. Noah trusted, obeyed, and feared the Lord (Heb. 11:7; Gen. 6:8–9:29); Abraham trusted when he didn't know what would happen (Heb. 11:8–10, 17–19; Gen. 12:1–4; 22:1–19); Sarah trusted when her circumstances seemed impossible (Heb. 11:11–12; Gen. 21:1–7); and Moses chose a path of suffering and ridicule rather than wealth and power (Heb. 11:23–28; Ex. 2:10–15). Each died in their faith— waiting for the promises to be fulfilled.

Hebrews 11:7–28 covers the period leading up to the flood to Abraham—-where the writer spends the most time—to the period of Exodus. From the patriarchs to the period of Exodus is approximately 4000 BC to 1445 BC. That is a massive period of time![12] Covenants, promises, miracles, and foreshadowing of Jesus sweep through these texts.

(Please note that although we will not explore the faith of Isaac, Jacob, and Joseph through the devotionals, you will study the verses in your main Bible study questions.)

---

12. Biblehub.com, the online reference mentioned in the "Studying the Bible" section of this study, has a quick reference guide of approximate dates for the Bible's timeline: https://biblehub.com/timeline/.

READ | HEBREWS 11:7–28

RESPOND

These are the core Bible study questions you'll work through this week:

1. What did Noah do by faith (Heb. 11:7; Gen. 6:8–9:29)?

2. Where in Hebrews have we seen the emphasis of things unseen?

3. How and where do we see judgment and salvation in the story of Noah? Write down specific words that signify these realities.

4. What did Abraham do by faith (Heb. 11:8–10; 17–19)?

5. What was the city Abraham was looking forward to (Heb. 11:10)?

6. What did Sarah do by faith?

7. Hebrews 6:14 refers to Abraham, citing Genesis 22:17. But Paul also references Abraham's faith in the midst of a failing body (Rom. 4:19). What do these verses say about God?

8. What does it mean that "all died in faith," and what are the things promised but not received (Heb. 11:13)?

9. Hebrews 11:10 and verses 14–16 parallel one another—what is the homeland?

10. "Therefore" signals that we need to look at the preceding verses. Why is God not ashamed (Heb. 11:16)?

11. What did Isaac, Jacob, and Joseph do by faith (Heb. 11:20–22)?

12. What did Moses do by faith (Heb. 11:23–28)?

13. How did the faith of his parents preserve him (Ex. 2:1–2)?

14. What is the reproach of Christ (Heb. 11:26)? By cross-referencing, where else in Scripture do you find this idea of receiving the reproach of Christ?

15. What is the reward (Heb. 11:26)?

16. What is the significance of Moses's participation in the Passover and faith? Why would it be an act of faith (Ex. 12:1–32)?

17. Where is Jesus in these verses? Where do you see the gospel?

18.   What do you learn about God and His character in these verses?

19.   How might you apply these verses to your life?

WEEK THREE | DAY ONE

EXPLORE

Reverent Faith: Noah

READ | HEBREWS 11:7; GENESIS 6:13–22

We begin our journey into the well-known faithful with perhaps one of the most known and retold stories in the Bible. Even Hollywood took time and money to adapt a comedy based on this biblical story. Because it's familiar, I won't take time to rehash it. But I do encourage you to read the account in Genesis in its entirety (Genesis, chapters 6–9). I want to instead focus on what the writer of Hebrews points out to us: Noah's reverent fear led to his faithful action.

Like Enoch, Noah walked with God—he had an intimate relationship with the Lord. He was a righteous man. He trusted God and it showed during a time that mattered greatly. God warned Noah of the impending destruction of the earth due to the unrighteousness of that generation and all of mankind. He instructed him to build an incredibly large ark, gather his family and animals, and stay in the boat. What's remarkable to me is that Moses simply records, "Noah did this; he did all that God commanded him" (Gen. 6:22; see also 7:5).

From all accounts, Noah did not question God. He simply obeyed. I don't know that I've ever just obeyed, especially when charged with an important mission. I imagine I'd ask questions. And there's nothing wrong with questions; asking God questions is not in opposition to loving Him. But Noah's response does reflect an awe, trust, worship, and faith that can be described as reverent fear. To do what Noah did and believe that the Lord would indeed save him and his family was a clear sign of faith in a sovereign and good God. We see Noah's reverent fear as he put his faith into action and did as God commanded.

That Noah feared the Lord is evident in the way he lived in a generation devoid of godliness. Noah was spared, but according to Peter, Noah was a "herald of righteousness" (2 Peter 2:5). A herald is one who brings good news. Therefore, Noah did not selfishly keep the news to himself; he didn't leave his generation to endure a flood without warning them. He warned them. It would take great boldness, love of neighbor, and faith in the Lord to speak the truth to a people opposed to the things of God. He feared the Lord more than he feared men.

REFLECT

1. How might God be calling you to step out in faith?

2. Have you ever considered the culture that Noah found himself in? What are ways that you might find yourself needing to speak the truth in love?

3. What is the fear of the Lord?

4. How does the fear of the Lord enable or ignite greater faith in the Lord?

WEEK THREE | DAY TWO

Faith in the Unknown: Abraham

READ | HEBREWS 11:8–10, 17–19; GENESIS 12:1–4; 22:1–19

It's rare for me to make decisions without knowing some aspect of what might come next. For example, if I'm asked to consider a job change, I might not know what the work environment will be like, but I'd investigate. I'd speak with other employees, research the business online, and consult with those closest to me before deciding. And if it's a situation that requires considerable loss, I'm likely to pass on it.

What Abraham was asked to do doesn't really compare to a job change, and clearly, these requests came from someone with considerably more . . . let's say, clout. But if I were to list situations I'd hope to avoid, I'd include: 1) leaving my support system, church, and extended family behind without any clear understanding of what that experience would be like, and 2) sacrificing one of my children for anything, no matter the reason. And these circumstances are the exact ones Abraham endured and in which he was found faithful.

Abraham lived a life of unknowns. First, in Genesis 12, Abraham—at the time called Abram[13]—was called by God to leave Haran and go to Canaan (vv. 1–4). Abraham was called away from everything he knew and held dear, including his land and parts of his family, to go to a foreign land. What's more is that God speaks of people who might dishonor him (v. 3). So, Abraham is going to a foreign

---

13. At times the Lord changes the names of His people to establish a new identity. Abram's name was changed to Abraham, which means "the father of a multitude of nations" and confirms the covenant He made with Abram (Gen. 17:4). I am using the name Abraham for consistency and because the writer of Hebrews 11 does.

land and may endure suffering at the hands of others. At this point, I'd likely say, thanks, but no thanks. But Abraham went—immediately.

Abraham doesn't place his faith in his abilities, wisdom, or strength. His faith is in the God who called him out into the foreign land. Abraham obeyed "not knowing where he was going," but he knew the One who was sending him (Heb. 11:8). But it wasn't blind faith. God did tell Abraham that He'd be with him and that Abraham would receive an inheritance (Gen. 12:2–3). He believed that God was a promise-keeping God. But, in my view, Abraham's ultimate test was with his son Isaac.

In summary, Abraham was asked to sacrifice his only son. That's more than I could imagine bearing. But when we understand the full context, that request seems even more unbearable. Our text in Hebrews, when cross-referenced, takes us to Genesis 22. To understand why Genesis 22 is a great test, we should read Genesis 17:15–21. God told Abraham that his wife Sarai would be called Sarah and she would be the mother of nations (v. 16). Sarah was not only barren, she was also ninety years old (Gen. 11:30)! Not to mention, Abraham was a hundred years old.

Sarah and Abraham did have a son, which was the fulfillment of God's promise to them and nothing short of a miracle (Gen. 21:1–2). Isaac was a gift to the older adults who longed for children.[14] Now Abraham was being asked to take his son, "your only son Isaac, whom you love," and sacrifice this gift (Gen. 22:2). So, Abraham proceeded to do just as the Lord had commanded. Similar to his obedience to go to the foreign land, Abraham had confidence that God would work in this situation.

Abraham went to sacrifice his only son but with the belief that he would return with his son (Gen. 22:5). He believed that God would raise Isaac from the dead, likely due to God's promise to Abraham in Genesis 21:12 that "through Isaac shall your offspring be named." Again, Abraham displayed faith in uncertain times. He didn't know what the future held, but he was sure that God would be with him and save his son.

---

14. In Genesis 16 we read about the devastating effect of not trusting the Lord. Sarai (later Sarah; see note 13) mistreated and abused her servant Hagar. Hagar bore a child with Abram after Sarai demanded it because of her barrenness. Unfortunately, Sarai became jealous, and Hagar fled after being mistreated by Sarai. However, the Lord saw Hagar and comforted her.

Abraham's faith is convicting! I have lacked faith for much lesser things than these. And although we should never compare ourselves to others, we can ask the Lord for grace to imitate Abraham's faith (1 Cor. 11:1). You and I may face many circumstances that will leave us uncertain about what to do. Let's remember the One who Abraham remembered as we walk out our faith in the unknown.

REFLECT

1. Have you ever experienced a situation where the general outcome was completely unknown?

2. What are some attributes of God that can help you in the face of uncertainty?

3. God was faithful to Abraham time and time again. So, there's a possibility that by the time we get to Isaac's potential sacrifice, Abraham could look back over his life and walk in faith as a result. How might remembering what the Lord did in other situations in the past help us as we face the future?

4. How do the promises of God, specifically as they relate to the gospel, help us as we face uncertainty?

WEEK THREE | DAY THREE

EXPLORE

Faith in the Impossible (or Faith When Things Seem Impossible): Sarah

READ | HEBREWS 11:11; GENESIS 17:19; 21:1–7

I remember that when I first got married I naively thought that getting pregnant, sustaining a pregnancy, and then delivering a child was like riding a bike. People seemed to do it with great ease all the time. At least, that's how it appeared. I didn't have a great many married friends, and the women I did have a relationship with didn't seem to reveal much about their private lives. It wasn't until I began having trouble getting pregnant and subsequently have two miscarriages that I realized how common infertility and miscarriages were. I ended up having a total of four miscarriages, but I did eventually give birth to our two children. Although I have children, when I read Sarah's story, there's much about her response that I can relate to, and I imagine the same will be true for you.

As has already been established, Sarah was barren. It can be assumed that she and Abraham attempted to bear children but were unable to conceive. But now, Sarah is old, and, biologically speaking, she would not be physically able to have children (Gen. 18:11). Sarah overheard the Lord discussing the pending pregnancy of Sarah, and she did what I think most in her state would do: she laughed in disbelief (v. 12).

This part of the story is quite remarkable to me. Sarah is confronted for laughing and denies it. Then the Lord calls her on the lie (vv. 13–15). She did laugh and she did struggle to believe that she could become pregnant. How can it be? And the Lord tells her and all of us, "Is anything too hard for the LORD?" (v. 14). God was incredibly gracious with her and reassured her faith. He didn't condemn her. It's such a picture of mercy and grace.

The writer in Hebrews points out that Sarah conceived and had faith not because her faith was incredible, but because she believed God was faithful: "She considered *him* faithful who had promised" (Heb. 11:11). God turns her laughter from doubt to joy (Gen. 21:6). She's amazed by the gracious gift of the Lord and the miraculous birth of Isaac (v. 7).

There are only two women featured in Hebrews 11 by name. Although I can't know for sure why the Lord chose this woman and this particular story, I can only imagine the many women who've heard and read about her story and were comforted. Although the Lord doesn't promise to do everything that we ask, He does promise to be faithful to us. He told Sarah that she would be pregnant. That pregnancy, by all earthly standards, was impossible, and the Lord did the impossible. Today, you and I may struggle to believe as Sarah did at first, but we can turn to the Lord and say, as He said to us, "What is impossible with man is possible with God" (Luke 18:27).

REFLECT

1. Have you ever been in a situation that seemed impossible? How have you seen the faithfulness of God in that situation?

2. The Lord highlights Sarah's faith even though she doubted. Why do you think it's good and helpful to know this aspect of Sarah's story?

3.   Are there any areas in your life that you now believe God can't handle? How might you take steps to surrender them to the Lord?

4.   It has been said that God is doing thousands of things on our behalf but we may only be aware of a few of them. Take a moment to recall, through sharing with a group, or writing them out, the different ways the Lord has been faithful to you.

WEEK THREE | DAY FOUR

Faith in the Promises

READ | HEBREWS 11:13–16

In the 1990s, I remember sitting by my boombox listening to popular songs on the radio, many of which were catchy, cheesy pop songs. As I was recently thinking about Abraham and Sarah, one of those songs popped in my head. The chorus expressed the desire to find "a place in this world."[15]

The fact that I had no idea that the song, "Place in this World," was written and sung by popular Christian artist Michael W. Smith is proof that I didn't grow up in an evangelical church (or any church for that matter). And although the song's meaning may not have been intended to reflect the idea of exile, I do think it encapsulates it.

Many of us sense that longing for a place as we navigate the Christian faith on this earth. It can feel like we are "roaming through the night." And sooner or later, it becomes clear that this earth is not our home. We're passing through a foreign land as we journey to our forever home.

Every Old Testament saint who put their faith in the Lord died in faith waiting for their Savior (Heb. 11:13). But for Abraham and Sarah, there were multiple promises that they had not yet received when they died. Abraham and Sarah obeyed the Lord and stepped out in faith and, in many ways, lived lives in waiting.

---

15. Wayne Kirkpatrick, Amy Grant, Michael W. Smith, "Place in This World," *Go West Young Man* (New York: BMG Studio, 1990), https://www.azlyrics.com/lyrics/michaelwsmith/placeinthisworld.html.

The writer highlights that they were exiles and strangers on this earth (v. 13). And they weren't figuratively foreigners—they were literally foreigners. Abraham and Sarah were promised to be the parents of a multitude of nations (that's quite a few kids). None of these things came to pass in their lifetime—they didn't receive the promised land, and they didn't see the many nations born from them. They both died believing that the Lord would make it so after they were gone. Abraham and Sarah's experience magnifies the experience of everyone who died before Jesus came to earth.

Although you and I have received the promised Savior, we too are in a season of waiting. That uneasiness you feel—maybe deep groaning—is a longing for heaven. We are waiting for Jesus to return. We, like the saints before, "desire a better country, that is, a heavenly one" (v. 16). We live in what theologians call the already, but not yet. The kingdom has come (already), but we await the glory to be revealed (not yet). So, we wait patiently for the Lord to return and make all things new.

The faith of the Old Testament saints is nothing short of miraculous. They all died not seeing Jesus. They all had faith in the promises of God. And you and I reflect their faith when we trust that God will do what He says He will do.

REFLECT

1. How does the idea of strangers and exiles apply to us today?

2. What is the city that they were seeking? From the Scriptures, find texts that help you understand what the city (heaven) will be like.

3.   What are some promises of God you can meditate on today?

4.   Why are His promises, which are true for us today, important, and how do they enable greater faith for the Christian walk?

WEEK THREE | DAY FIVE

A Life of Faith: Moses

READ | HEBREWS 11:23–28; EXODUS CHAPTERS 1 AND 2

There are many times when I sit down to listen to a friend as she shares her struggles that I think, *Although I'm not in that circumstance, I can relate to her general experience.* I don't generally state that because saying it isn't always helpful. And, of course, I don't relate in every way—only Jesus does. However, temptations and many circumstances are often common to most people. But when I read about the life of Moses, there's little at face value that I could imagine any of us relating to.

There would be no way to cover all of the events in the life of Moses, but here is a short overview of some featured in Hebrews 11:23–28: At the time of Moses's birth, the king of Egypt felt threatened by Israel and issued an order for the midwives to kill any son born to a Hebrew woman. The midwives didn't comply because they feared the Lord. So, Pharaoh ordered his people to cast the male babies into the Nile (Ex. 1:15–17, 22). Moses was born during this time, and his mom, a Jewish woman, hid him from Pharaoh so he would not be killed.

There came a time when Moses could no longer be hidden, so his mother, accompanied by his sister, put him in a basket to hide him on the riverbank of the Nile. This is where the birth and early childhood of Moses gets wild. Pharaoh's daughter went to the bank of the river to bathe and noticed the basket. Moses's sister approached the woman, which would have been risky, given that Moses's sister was one of the outcasts. She asked if she could assist the woman in finding someone to nurse the child. Pharaoh's daughter agreed, and so the sister went to get their mother. In the end, Moses's mom ends up getting paid to nurse her son (Ex. 2:3–9).

As the adopted son of Pharaoh's daughter, Moses lived a lavish life, free from the threat of slavery as was common for the Hebrews, and with enormous privileges. However, as Moses grew, so did his burden for his people (the Hebrews). At one point, Moses even killed an Egyptian, intervening to protect a Hebrew as the Egyptian beat the man. Pharaoh found out about this and sought to kill Moses. Moses fled (Ex. 2:11–15).

These are only a few areas of the beginning of Moses's life that are highlighted by the writer of Hebrews . . . and what a life! But in Hebrews 11, we see an incredible aspect of his faith, one that we all might face if we proclaim Jesus. Moses denied his adopted status and material positions—those were fleeting pleasures—and instead *chose* to be mistreated (Heb. 11:25). His faith was great because of what he did in adversity for the cause of the Lord (Heb. 11:26).

We may not have the same experiences as Moses, but we can share in his faith in the face of rejection and by shining a light on our allegiance to Jesus. Moses's action would have been countercultural. You and I will surely be in a situation where we'll need to decide if Jesus is worth being shunned by our coworkers, family, and community. As singer/songwriter Andrew Peterson eloquently sings, "Is He worthy? He is!"[16]

---

16. Ben Shive, Andrew Peterson, "Is He Worthy?," *Resurrection Letters, Vol. 1* (Nashville: Centricity Music, 2018), https://www.azlyrics.com/lyrics/andrewpeterson/isheworthy.html.

REFLECT

1. We can't overlook the bravery of all the women surrounding the beginning of Moses's life. How might God be calling you to live bravely on behalf of others?

2. Moses too showed compassion on his people and defended the oppressed. Although we should never take justice into our own hands and become vigilantes, there are ways we can exercise justice on the earth. What are practical ways you can pursue justice for others?

3. What might God be calling you to sacrifice for the sake of Christ?

4. How does the reproach Moses endured for his people reflect Jesus?

A Faith That Points to Jesus

There are several reasons for pausing to spend a week learning about Rahab and the Lord she trusted in. Sarah, Rahab, and Moses's mother are the only women featured in Hebrews 11. Sarah is mentioned alongside Abraham, and Moses's mother appears only briefly; therefore, Rahab has the distinction of being the only woman featured singularly and without question.[17]

Two remarkable facts stand out about Rahab: 1) she was a prostitute, and 2) she is in the lineage of Jesus. But what stood out to the author of Hebrews was her faith. She was an unlikely heroine and helped secure the spies, instructed them, and ultimately assisted in the fall of Jericho. She did as the spies cautioned and saved her whole household. She trusted the Lord; and her story also highlights the amazing grace bestowed on all people, regardless of their sin, by our Lord and Savior.

READ | HEBREWS 11:30–31; JOSHUA 2; 6:17–25

---

17. Some argue that Sarah's mention is a digression and the subject of the faith remains on Abraham. Therefore, the writer of Hebrews did not intend to feature her faith but rather mention her in light of the whole story of Isaac's birth. F. F. Bruce, *The Epistle to the Hebrews* (Grand Rapids, MI: Eerdmans, 1990), 294–95. Note—I believe from the text we can affirm Sarah's faith and that the writer intended to highlight it in light of the words "by faith" and the details of her faith. But this is part of the joy and mystery of reading various interpretations and coming to one's own conclusion.

RESPOND

These are the core Bible study questions you'll work through this week:

1. Whose faith led to the walls of Jericho falling down (Heb. 11:30; Josh. 6:1–21)? Hebrews 11:30 helps establish some context for Rahab's story.

2. What did Rahab do by faith (Heb. 11:31)?

3. What can you glean about Rahab (culture, ethnicity, etc.) from Joshua 2? Why is her background significant in this situation?

4. James uses Rahab to make a case that "faith apart from works is dead" (James 2:25–26). What specifically does she do that is zeroed in on and how is that "works"?

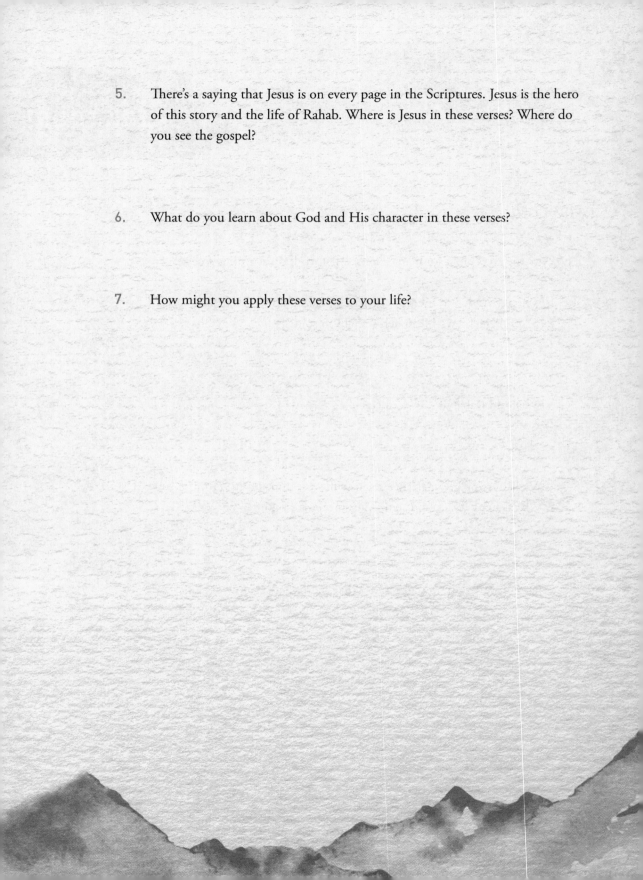

5.   There's a saying that Jesus is on every page in the Scriptures. Jesus is the hero of this story and the life of Rahab. Where is Jesus in these verses? Where do you see the gospel?

6.   What do you learn about God and His character in these verses?

7.   How might you apply these verses to your life?

WEEK FOUR | DAY ONE

Amazing Grace

READ | HEBREWS 11:31; JOSHUA 2:1

I became a Christian at the age of 22. I would have been considered a "good girl" by worldly standards but I had a dating problem. I didn't date many boys, but the ones I did were long, serious relationships. A long, serious relationship as a non-Christian generally means there's not much as to convictions and the fear of the Lord holding you back. But God was gracious to save me and forgive all my sin. This became my anthem song: "Amazing grace, how sweet the sound that saved a wretch like me. I once was lost but now I'm found, was blind but now I see."[18]

The same amazing grace that is available to me is the same amazing grace that is available to you, and it's the same amazing grace Rahab experienced.

In Hebrews 11:31, the Lord chose to remind us again that Rahab was a prostitute. He could have set that part of her history aside and focused on her treatment of the spies without any reference to her sinful occupation. It might seem perplexing. Aren't we new creations once we are saved? Should we be reminded of our past sin? But I don't believe that it was mentioned to remind us about her sin at all. As a matter of fact, I don't think it was about her. Rather, I believe it's to point our attention to Him.

---

18. See John Newton, "Amazing Grace," 1779.

The story of Rahab is a story of God's glorious, cosmic, undeserving grace toward a Gentile sinner and her people. Along with grace, we see mercy. He could have executed judgment, but instead He had compassion. Rahab's story doesn't end once the spies leave her place. We see her show up in the most unlikely place: the genealogy of Jesus Christ (Matt. 1:5).

Had you or I written this text, I imagine we would have figured out a way to remove the reference to a prostitute—it's too dirty for the Bible, we might think. Even commentary writers have attempted to edit her description.[19] As I continue to learn about the mercy and grace of God, the more I'm thankful God is not like you and me. We are slow to forgive and really slow to forget. We hold sin against one another, remembering it in our thoughts, bringing it up in our hearts. But not so for the Lord. He does not hold our sin against us. He's reminding us in this text that He's not ashamed to be associated with sinners. He's not ashamed to associate with you or with me.

REFLECT

1.   Have you ever wondered why the Lord would use the descriptor *prostitute*[20] even after she's found in this list? What does it tell you about the Lord?

2.   When you think about your testimony, are there areas in your life that you struggle to face because of shame? What about the story of Rahab and the character of God help you with shame?

---

19. "2. Preparing to Enter the Land (Joshua 2:1–24)," Bible.org, https://bible.org/seriespage/preparing-enter-land-joshua-21-24.
20. Some scholars believe that Rahab was likely trafficked and sold into prostitution but because of her place in society—powerless and female—she chose to remain a prostitute. See Carolyn Custis James, "Tamar: The Righteous Prostitute," in *Vindicating the Vixens: Revisiting Sexualized, Vilified, and Marginalized Women of the Bible*, ed. Sandra L. Glahn (Grand Rapids, MI: Kregel Academic, 2017), 40–41.

3.   Is there any area of your life you haven't surrendered to the Lord? How does Rahab's experience encourage you to go to the Lord in repentance?

4.   Although we are not in the genealogy of Christ, we are a part of His family. How does the reality of being a part of His family build your faith?

WEEK FOUR | DAY TWO

EXPLORE

God's Plan in Unconventional Methods

READ | HEBREWS 11:31; JOSHUA 2:2–4

I have a friend who is an ethicist and professor of ethics. I've heard that every year in one of his seminars he gives an almost impossible ethical situation for the students to work through. As someone who thinks in categories of black and white and right and wrong, it's hard sometimes to see the grey. I don't tend to believe in "necessary evils." But life isn't always that cut-and-dried. There are times when God uses the sin of others to advance His purposes. This is the case with Rahab and the spies.

At the beginning of the book of Joshua, Joshua is given instructions to enter the Land of Promise (Josh. 1). This would not be an easy task—he would need to take the land that was promised by the Lord to Israel. Now I've never tried to invade and occupy land (some things go without saying), but I do imagine that in order to do it, you'd need to know what you are walking into. Joshua sent two spies to the city of Jericho to gain intelligence before charging ahead.

The two spies left and went to Rahab's home to stay (Josh. 2:1). As you read the narrative, you see that there's no reason to believe that they engaged in anything inappropriate with Rahab. The spies were on a mission, and Rahab's home was likely a place where sojourners could stay, which would make sense given they knew to go to her home. Their secret location was not safe in that area, and their whereabouts were made known to the king of Jericho (v. 3). And this is where our ethical dilemma begins.

Rahab hid the spies, but it was told to the king of Jericho. The king sent for Rahab—confronting her and charging her to bring out the two men (v. 3). Rahab responded, "True, the men came to me, but I did not know where they were from. And when the gate was about to be closed at dark, the men went out. I do not know where the men went. Pursue them quickly, for you will overtake them" (vv. 4–5).

She lied. No need to mince words or pretend it's not in the text. Rahab lied to the king to protect the spies. That is clear and rather easy to conclude. The hard thing is to determine whether or not her lying was acceptable.

Nowhere where Rahab is mentioned in the Bible is there any attention brought to her lie (Heb. 11:31; James 2:25). Her faith and obedience are the highlights of her life. Those aspects of her life are remembered and should be emulated. Also, nowhere do we see her lie celebrated. It is simply a part of the narrative story—meant to help us understand the historical nature of the events. But also, don't believe the Lord adds details willy-nilly. There have been other episodes where deception was used to fulfill the purposes of the Lord.[21] So, what might we learn from this?

As I read Rahab's amazing story about her strength and her faith in the midst of terrifying circumstances (her city is about to be destroyed!), I can't help but thank the Lord that salvation is by grace alone, through faith alone (Eph. 2:8–9). You and I are not saved by our good deeds, our perfect performance, or anything we might think we could contribute. None of our sin is overlooked (we have been bought with a price), but any righteousness we have belongs to Christ (1 Cor. 6:20; Rom. 3:22). That doesn't mean we go on sinning, by no means (Rom. 6:1–2). But it does mean we thank the Lord for His mercy and grace during moments of uncertainty as we try to honor Him in all we do.

---

21. See Exodus 1:15–21; 1 Samuel 16:2; and 1 Kings 22:19–23.

REFLECT

1. This is a narrative, and we shouldn't draw strict conclusions such as those found in Paul's letters. The text itself never comments on the ethics of her actions. Have you ever considered that Rahab lied to protect the spies? What are your initial thoughts considering the situation?

2. What are other situations where an ethical dilemma might be experienced in our lifetime? (Example: hiding a victim of abuse, etc.)

3. When I read the text, I see the mercy of God. What other aspects of God's character might you see in this story?

4. If every detail of our life were written out for the world to see, I imagine we'd have areas that we'd need to ask for forgiveness. Although the text doesn't condemn or affirm Rahab's actions, it does bring out deception. Are there areas in your life where you might need to confess? How does remembering her faith encourage yours?

WEEK FOUR | DAY THREE

Knowing God Leads to Faith

READ | HEBREWS 11:31; JOSHUA 2:9–11

After I became a Christian, I was zealous about the Lord. I loved reading my Bible and fellowshipping with God through prayer. One day, I said something that wasn't clear—I don't remember what I said exactly, but I'll never forget the response of one of the people sitting with me. The woman replied, "Do you even know the gospel?" Her words cut deep, but they also filled me with fear. What if I thought I knew the Lord but I didn't? What if I didn't know how to even explain the basics of the faith I professed?

So, I started studying, and I learned everything I could. I read theology books and built up as much knowledge as possible. And I became puffed up and critical of those who didn't believe the way I did. Thankfully, this was before I began writing publicly. The Lord revealed my growing arrogance by growing my love for His Word and desire to get to know Him more. The more I learned, the more I saw (and continue to see) how much I still had to learn. I would soon take this new desire and put it into action through evangelism and campus ministry.

You might be wondering—how is this about Rahab? It is. Stay with me. J. I. Packer wrote in *Knowing God* that, "one can know a good deal about God without much knowledge of him."[22] Rahab knew a great deal about God and the history of Israel. Let's take a look at Joshua 2:9–11:

---

22. J. I. Packer, *Knowing God* (Downers Grove, IL: InterVarsity, 1973), 26.

"I know that the LORD has given you the land, and that the fear of you has fallen upon us, and that all the inhabitants of the land melt away before you. For we have heard how the LORD dried up the water of the Red Sea before you when you came out of Egypt, and what you did to the two kings of the Amorites who were beyond the Jordan, to Sihon and Og, whom you devoted to destruction. And as soon as we heard it, our hearts melted, and there was no spirit left in any man because of you, for the LORD your God, he is God in the heavens above and on the earth beneath."

It's actually remarkable how much Rahab knew given her background and personal history (Gentile and prostitute). She had heard and paid attention. But more than that, she believed deep in her heart. Rahab knew more about God and His greatness than I'm sure even the spies could have imagined. Her knowledge led to worship and the fear of the Lord.

J. I. Packer warns that "if we pursue theological knowledge for its own sake, it is bound to go bad on us. It will make us proud and conceited."[23] Although we do not know when Rahab came to believing faith, she not only understood God's covenant with Abraham and what would happen to Jericho, she spoke of God's greatness. But again, anyone could say these things—even demons know about the Lord and shudder (James 2:19). But her knowledge led her to faithful action. Her knowledge of God led her to act bravely and help the spies, and her trust in God led her to plead for her family (Josh. 2:12–14).

REFLECT

1.   Why do you think knowledge has the potential to puff up?

---

23. J. I. Packer, *Knowing God* (Downers Grove, IL: InterVarsity, 1973), 21.

2. What should our response to knowledge be?

3. What is the fear of the Lord? Why might knowledge of God lead to the fear of the Lord?

4. How might trusting in the promises of God lead to greater faith?

WEEK FOUR | DAY FOUR

EXPLORE

And Faith Leads to Action

READ | HEBREWS 11:31; JOSHUA 2:12–14

Today's devotional is an extension of Week Four, Day Three. We ended thinking about how Rahab's knowledge of God led her to faithful action. We've been exploring various aspects of her action, but today, let's take a look at the action highlighted by the writer of Hebrews.

How we treat others matters. But have you ever considered that how you treat someone could be evidence of where you put your faith? Think about how you've responded after someone sinned against you. Did you trust the Lord to avenge for you, or did you hold a grudge, retaliate, or gossip? How we respond reveals where our hearts are resting and where they are bent. We won't get this right all of the time, but it can prove our faith to be true faith.

If faith without works is dead, then how we treat others proves our faith to be true. At least that's what James wrote as he referenced Rahab in James 2:24–26. James used Rahab as an example for what it looks like to put our faith into action. He wrote:

> You see that a person is justified by works and not by faith alone. And in the same way was not also Rahab the prostitute justified by works when she received the messengers and sent them out by another way? For as the body apart from the spirit is dead, so also faith apart from works is dead.

Rahab had a choice to make when those spies came to see her. She could let them in or—given what she knew was about to happen to her city and her people—she could have refused or reported it to the king. She chose to take all her knowledge about God and believe that He had the power to save her family. She extended hospitality to the spies and welcomed them into her place (Heb. 11:31). She offered a friendly welcome—serving them in every way. Her faith in God, her fear of the Lord, and her belief in the promises of God led her to act counterculturally in every way.

REFLECT

1. It can be hard to step out in faith in circumstances that are relatively simple. Rahab's situation was tough. Have you ever had to trust the Lord and do something hard but good?

2. James 2:26 is one of the most debated texts in Scripture. But when paired with the example of Rahab as James does, it's a refreshing reminder that our actions provide proof of what the Lord has already done. Have you ever noticed the examples of Rahab (and Abraham!) as examples of faith in action?

3. Rahab's treatment of the spies (kindness) wasn't an act; otherwise, she wouldn't have been recorded in Hebrews in such a way. How might her knowledge of God have helped her extend kindness to the spies?

4.   How does our knowledge of God help us to act likewise to others?

WEEK FOUR | DAY FIVE

EXPLORE

A Cord That Leads to Jesus

READ | HEBREWS 11:31; JOSHUA 2:17–21

It has been said that a scarlet cord runs throughout the Bible. This phrase can be summed up basically as all roads lead to Jesus. The Old Testament to the New Testament is ultimately about Jesus. Writing about the relationship between the Old Testament and the New Testament, pastor Burk Parsons writes:

> That doesn't mean, however, that Jesus is hiding under every stone in the Old Testament, nor does it mean that we need to overturn every stone in our pursuit to find Him at the cost of sound exegesis. Nevertheless, it does mean that every stone points to Christ and beckons us to examine the manifold ways in which Christ is in the foreground and background of the landscape of every stone in all the Scriptures, by God's sovereign orchestration and for our redemption in Christ, who is the same yesterday, today, and forever.[24]

In the story of Rahab, Jesus is there in the foreground and background of the landscape and specifically in the salvation of Rahab and her entire family.

Rahab requested that the spies deal with her family as she had dealt with them: kindly (Josh. 2:12). They agreed and directed her to tie a scarlet cord in the window where she lowered the men and to stay inside the home with her family until they passed over her home (vv. 17–21). These instructions are similar to the first Passover found in Exodus 12:22.

---

24. Burk Parsons, "The Christ of the Old and New," Ligonier Ministries, https://www.ligonier.org/learn/articles/christ-old-and-new.

Interestingly, nowhere in the text is there any explicit mention of a Messiah, and commentaries—at least the ones I've read—don't draw a great deal of attention to this scarlet rope. So, as much as I want to say, "See, look, it's about Jesus!" I hesitate to make such a declaration. But then again, it sure seems to point us to our Savior—their coming Savior.

The scarlet thread, or in this case a rope, seems symbolic of the Lamb of God who would one day take away the sin of the world (John 1:29). Rahab was "passed over" and spared because of this rope foreshadowing the Lord's work of forgiveness of our sin because of the death of Jesus. Unlike Rahab, there isn't anything we must do or sacrifice or give up, for Jesus did what we could not do.

> For what the law was powerless to do because it was weakened by the flesh, God did by sending his own Son in the likeness of sinful flesh to be a sin offering. (Rom. 8:3 NIV)

And for this we say, thank You, Jesus!

REFLECT

1. Have you heard that Jesus is on every page of Scripture? How have you seen this in other Bible stories? If you haven't, what might be other ways you see it here in the story of Rahab?

2. Thinking back to what we studied the first week, how does the symbolism here of the first Passover in Rahab's story foreshadow the Messiah?

3. Why would it be important to remind our hearts again that Christ's sacrifice was enough?

4. Rahab's faith saved her entire family. Although the text doesn't share a word about what her conversations were like with her family, one has to wonder. It's not a leap to imagine she shared all that she knew about God, the history of Israel, and the promises of God. And we already know that her legacy includes Jesus! How might our faith impact those around us?

The Powerful and Faithful

Gideon, Barak, Samson, Jephthah, David, Samuel, and the prophets.

The two verses in today's reading are some of the most unique in Hebrews 11. The writer has run out of space and time to continue and begins listing men in, what appears to be, random order. As we'll see, all of these men have failed in some way—from cowardice to murder! Yet in the text we do not see their sins and failures even mentioned. They are remembered for their faith and trust in God. The implications for us should bring great freedom and joy. Not freedom to sin; rather, peace in knowing our perseverance and faithfulness isn't based on our personal track record, but on Christ's.

But those men listed weren't all whom the writer referenced. He also referenced characteristics of those who had faith. Similar to the writer of Hebrews who expressed that there would be no way to write all of the faithful, we can't cover every king, judge, and prophet here. As it is with all Bible study, there are yet depths to reach, and I encourage you to dive deeper still.

READ | HEBREWS 11:32–34

RESPOND

These are the core Bible study questions you'll work through this week:

Our author asked a rhetorical question before explaining that he was out of time (Heb. 11:32). He then gave us a list of names but also includes "the prophets." What can be safely deduced from this is that there are many faithful who are not named. Because of this lack of detail, this week you will search through the Scriptures to discover some of the faithful who might have been featured in this book based on the characteristics our writer described. You'll be cross-referencing Hebrews with the rest of the Old Testament to create this list. However, I have provided names and stories based on my research for us to study together in the devotionals.

1.   List the names the writer mentioned in Hebrews 11:32.

2.   List the characteristics that made them faithful (vv. 32–34).

3.   Match these men to the characteristics. Note that in verse 32, the writer includes "the prophets." Using cross references, who are others who fit the descriptions? The men listed by name do not all fit each description.

4.   Find as many of their stories in the Scriptures as possible. (To get you started, this is a great opportunity to refer to the chart at the beginning of the study.)

5.   Many of these men had powerful positions; they also failed in various ways. Where is Jesus in these verses? Where do you see the gospel?

6.   What do you learn about God and His character in these verses?

7.   How might you apply these verses to your life?

WEEK FIVE | DAY ONE

EXPLORE

Too Many to Name

READ | HEBREWS 11:32

As we get to the end of the chapter, the writer stops sharing specific names and occasions of faithfulness and begins instead to list judges, prophets, and a king in random order (not in order of historical or biblical appearance). It's not that these men were not important; on the contrary, they are indeed important. It is instead just as the author noted, "For time would fail me to tell of . . ." (Heb. 11:32). For the sake of brevity, the writer listed various triumphs or circumstances that each person endured and that required faith.

There's something oddly comforting to me in those words. Just as we found encouragement in how the Lord noticed the obscure figure of Enoch, we can be encouraged that the Lord sees all of us. This list in Hebrews 11 is indeed the great Hall of Faith, but it isn't comprehensive. Think about some of the most faithful men and women not mentioned in this list such as Deborah, Ruth, Job, Daniel . . . the list could go on and on. All of these are people who died in faith—not seeing the ultimate, promised King (v. 13). But the list of faithful could stretch on for centuries.

Another encouraging aspect about the list is that it isn't meant to be hierarchical. The next devotional will delve into the specific people mentioned in verse 32, and what we quickly see is that none of these people was close to exemplary in their faith—on the contrary, many failed miserably. But they are not the only ones on this list who had failed. Abraham could be deceitful (Gen. 12:10–20); Sarah was jealous (Gen. 16:4–6); Noah was drunk (Gen. 9:20–29); Rahab, as we know, was a prostitute; and even Moses's mistake of faithlessness meant he could not enter the promised land (Num. 20).

All of these people are not meant to be idolized, and they don't comprise an exhaustive list of those who were perfect. No one is perfect but our Lord (Rom. 3:23). The Hall of Faith is meant to give us examples of the enduring faith of believers through their failures and through their trials, and it is meant to point us to the faithfulness of God.

Aren't we glad this isn't an exhaustive list? Aren't we happy that God provided His perfect Son for imperfect faithfulness? And aren't we glad that it is not our good works that allow us to be in the Lamb's Book of Life (Rev. 20:15)? You will be called faithful because our God is faithful.

REFLECT

1. Does it build your faith that the list of the faithful could go on and on and on? If so, why?

2. What character in the list do you relate most to and why?

3. What modern day "heroes of the faith" might you identify with and desire to emulate? (In the next week we will explore martyrs. Those are the saints I most want to emulate as their faith is sure and strong to the very end. If I can have faith in the face of persecution, I can have faith in the everyday stuff of life. I hope you enjoy answering this question and thanking the Lord for those who have gone before us.)

4. Often some of the most faithful men and women are unknown. Who are you looking to in your local context and why? (If you've never shared how their faith inspires you, take time to do it this week. Your encouragement is also one application of Hebrews 10:24–25.)

EXPLORE

A Life of Failures

READ | HEBREWS 11:32–34

As a young girl, every time we'd receive a newspaper, I'd go straight to the obituaries. Looking back, it seems like such an odd habit for a teenager. I was fascinated with the lives of those who died. I didn't know any of them personally, but I wanted to know everything about them. It would make sense that later in life I would end up writing for a newspaper in the features section—I was always interested in people and their stories. The obituaries gave me a glimpse into what others thought about their loved ones.

Obituaries are usually a way to note the good things about a person. It is rare that there's a negative obituary that shines light into all of the ugliness of a person's life. At the end of my life, I pray I'm not remembered for all the ways that I've failed the Lord, although there are many. Rather, I pray I'm remembered as being faithful.

Hebrews 11:32–34 reads like an obituary, except with the names lumped together. We get a list of names or categories of people (such as the prophets), and then a list of courageous, faith-filled acts of obedience and the dangers each person or group faced—but again, in list form and not specific to each individual. We know that some conquered kingdoms, enforced justice, obtained promises . . . and these things were part of what made them faithful. And just like when we read an obituary, we only get the highlight reel.

A closer look at the specific names mentioned—Gideon, Barak, Samson, Jephthah, David, Samuel, and the prophets—and we see that these heroes of the faith have very hard stories. The various stories included anything from deceit and fear to murder and idolatry.

Some theologians even accuse the writer of Hebrews as presenting an "idealized view" of the judges mentioned in this list.[25] Their lives were not ones of consistent faith or faithfulness. And although none of us will likely build an object that causes an entire people to worship an idol (looking at you, Gideon), all of us in some way have been unfaithful to the Lord too.

I can think of several women I admire because of their humility, faithfulness, grace, gentleness, courage, and tenacity. I know none of the women on my list are perfect, not one. They are faithful. Now if I dug deep enough into the crevices of their hearts and minds, I might find all manner of sin. At the end of our days, the only thing that will matter is that we are found in Jesus. Some of the most faithful people I know also include some of the hardest stories of redemption.

If your life has been in ruins, God is not done with you. He is not. It may feel like the end of the road, but God promises to finish the good work He started in you (Phil. 1:6). He is not finished. He who calls us to faithfulness will give us the grace to endure. He who calls us faithful is faithful.

REFLECT

1. Given the unfaithfulness of many of those listed in this chapter, what can we learn about the character of God?

---

25. *ESV Study Bible*, ed. Wayne Grudem (Wheaton, IL: Crossway, 2008), note in the Introduction of Judges, 435. For further study of the life and the fall of many of these leaders, you can read the following: Gideon (Judg. 6:36–40); Samson (Judg. 13:7; 14–16; Num. 6:1–21 and many more); and David (2 Sam. 11–24).

2.   How can the gospel be applied to the way we live? And what are some gifts God gives to help us walk in faithfulness?

3.   What aspects of the characters' faith listed in verses 32–34 can we learn from and imitate?

4.   What do you hope you'll be remembered for?

WEEK FIVE | DAY THREE

EXPLORE

Made Strong in Weakness: Gideon

READ | HEBREWS 11:32–34; JUDGES 6–8

The writer of Hebrews highlights characteristics that made the Old Testament saints faithful. One of those characteristics is one we can all relate to. I have never met a person who hasn't felt weak or unsure at some point in their life. This is an almost universal experience, even when we account for the fact that our circumstances are so different. Gideon found himself in a terrifying circumstance that would require a great deal of faith in the all-powerful God.

In Judges 6, we see that Israel had been conquered by the Midianites because of the Hebrew people's disobedience and apostasy. Israel asked the Lord for deliverance, but the Lord sent a prophet who condemned them (vv. 1–10). Israel was in a desperate place. But then the Lord called Gideon to do what seemed like the impossible: defeat the Midianites. This is not a story of smooth sailing after God called him to act. Gideon was afraid of the Midianites and wasn't afraid to let the Lord know.

An angel of the Lord came to Gideon and said, "The LORD is with you, O mighty man of valor" (v. 12). Gideon responded by asking why, if God was with them, hadn't He rescued them? Then the angel told him to "go in this might of yours and save Israel" (v. 14). Two times the angel told Gideon he was mighty. Perplexed, Gideon let the Lord know—as if He didn't already know—that he was weak and his clan was weak. So the Lord told him again that He would be with him. But Gideon did not trust the Lord, at first. Instead, he asked the Lord for a sign (vv. 17–18). The Lord gave him more signs, and an army of 32,000 men, which God, Himself, reduced (7:2–8), leaving Gideon with only three hundred men for the great battle.

Gideon had two problems: he really did have a small army that he expected would be wiped out fairly quickly, and Gideon lacked faith because he was weak. On a human level, Gideon's responses make sense. We've all likely felt the tension between looking at reality and hoping for a miracle. There are times when a problem seems too big to me, and I'm fully aware of my weakness. *How in the world could this work out?* I wish I could say that I trust in the Lord's strength and have faith during every trouble. But, sometimes, I take things into my own hands; and sometimes, I shrink back in fear. Neither are the answer. Gideon took things into his own hands, making the Lord prove His faithfulness. And the Lord said to him, as He says to all of us, "But I will be with you" (6:16).

The Lord honored Gideon's request for a sign, but that didn't end Gideon's hesitation. Gideon asked the Lord to prove it again! I don't know if I've read a story in the Word that displays the patience of the Lord more than this. Gideon did not trust the promises God had already spoken to him. But God had a plan, and using Gideon was part of that plan. In an act of great mercy and patience, the Lord proved Himself again and fulfilled Gideon's request (vv. 36–40).

In the end, Gideon and his three hundred men did defeat Midian. Although Gideon was hesitant, his story is also a reminder that faith takes action (just as with Rahab). Gideon did test God (twice), but he eventually acted. Just because we are initially hesitant to act doesn't mean we can't be faithful going forward. Gideon proved to be faithful because he completed the task the Lord assigned him. He was made strong out of weakness.

Gideon, in this situation, represents all of us. None of us are strong in and of ourselves. You and I are dependent on God to finish our task—to even start our day. We need the Lord for every breath and every step we take. But this is especially true when we are doing any work to advance the cause of Christ. And when we truly recognize our weakness, it is then we can say: "For the sake of Christ, then, I am content with weaknesses, insults, hardships, persecutions, and calamities. For when I am weak, then I am strong" (2 Cor. 12:10).

REFLECT

1. Have you ever been in a situation where your weakness was incredibly apparent and you didn't know what to do?

2. What might it look like to test the Lord or ask Him for proof today?

3. How does knowing God will be with you through anything help your faith in uncertain times?

4. Can you think of other situations in Scripture or other texts where the Lord reminds His people of His faithfulness and presence in times of trouble?

EXPLORE

Stopped the Mouth of Lions: Daniel

READ | HEBREWS 11:32–34; DANIEL 6:16–28

Right now, the world is going through a terrible pandemic. I recently read a newsletter where my friend took note of the difference between this time we are in and other crises. What makes this situation unique is that it isn't isolated to one country or region. Every country *in the world* is being affected by a virus and almost every economy is shutting down as a result.

Occasionally I find my chest tightening and throat closing. It's a sort of physical form of anxiety that I've never experienced before. And occasionally, I'll remember to pray and ask the Lord to help me breathe and trust Him. Those moments when I remember the Lord and go to Him in prayer are the moments when my body settles—He is with me in this storm. He is all-powerful and all-knowing. I can surrender all the unknowns to Him.

I wish I could say that I was consistent and fervent in prayer in the unknown. I've spent more time in the news than I have on my face before the Lord. But there is someone, besides our Savior, who understood what it meant to have everything stacked against him while remaining consistent in prayer, faithfully entrusting his situation to God. Daniel was steadfast in prayer, as he had always been, in the face of accusations and a death sentence.

In Daniel 6, we see that a king named Darius set up regional leaders throughout the kingdom and three presidents over those regional leaders. Daniel was one of the presidents appointed by the king. Daniel excelled at his job, and the king sought to promote him over the entire kingdom (Dan. 6:1–3). Daniel's rise and recognition made the other leaders jealous and they conspired to find a way to disqualify him (vv. 4–5).

Their plot worked. They requested a new law that no one could make a petition to any god or man except the king (in effect, a temporary ban on prayer). Darius agreed to it and signed it into law, not knowing that it was a devious plot against his favored leader (vv. 6–9). The punishment for breaking this law was death by being thrown into a den of lions.

This is where Daniel's faith shined brightest. He learned of this law, but it did not stop him from continuing his practice of prayer—he prayed and gave thanks to the Lord as he had always done (v. 10). He didn't hide his faith in God even when he knew that it could lead to his death. Well, we know what happened next. Daniel was caught and reported and sentenced to death.

Daniel was cast into the den. Interestingly, the king points Daniel to the very God he was being punished for worshiping. He said, "May your God, whom you serve continually, deliver you!" (v. 16). The king noticed Daniel's continual leaning on the Lord. Oh, that you and I who know Jesus would be known as those who lean continually on the Lord! During the night the king could barely sleep as he worried about Daniel. Daniel, however, was secure in the arms of the Lord. The Lord had shut the lions' mouths (v. 22).

There are so many lessons we could learn from this story. But Hebrews 11:33 reminds us that in the face of a lion, Daniel had faith and believed God could save him. Daniel didn't pray because he knew what God was going to do. He had no idea. He prayed because he knew the God who could do it. No matter the circumstance, we can turn to God in prayer. As R. C. Sproul wrote in his book *Knowing Scripture*: "The issue of faith is not so much whether we believe in God, but whether we believe the God we believe in."[26]

---

26. R. C. Sproul, *Knowing Scripture* (Downers Grove, IL: InterVarsity, 1977), 30.

REFLECT

1. There are several different circumstances Daniel found himself in, including but not limited to: 1) Jealous leaders and vicious plots, 2) Deceitfulness, and 3) Submission to state versus submission to God. But his response to it all was the same. What aspect of the Lord's character do you believe Daniel clung to and how can you cling also?

2. If we fall into a den of lions, we may be devoured. God doesn't always save people as we will see in the verses ahead (Heb. 11:36–38). What could be dangerous about believing we didn't have enough faith to save ourselves?

3. What are practical ways you can incorporate prayer into your day?

4. How does knowing that Jesus lives to make intercession for us change the way you pray (Heb. 7:25; Rom. 8:34)?

WEEK FIVE | DAY FIVE

EXPLORE

Through the Fire: Shadrach, Meshach, and Abednego

READ | HEBREWS 11:32–34; DANIEL 3

Recently, I was a part of an event, and I stuck out like a sore thumb. Among the speakers, I was the only African American, the only woman, and the one who didn't seem to have a doctorate. The Lord continually takes me to places where I never thought I'd be. This is not a complaint—it's a reality and one that I've come to embrace. I thank God that I get to proclaim Him in various contexts, even if it's just in a board meeting.

But this feeling I often experience is a lot like the Christian life—alien. Instead, we are strangers in a land moving further and further away from God. We will all, at some point, be faced with the choice: proclaim Jesus or shrink back in fear. If we proclaim Him, we may look foolish to our peers or, in some places, experience physical harm because of our faith. Let the story of Shadrach, Meshach, and Abednego inspire us to have courage under fire.

King Nebuchadnezzar made an image of gold and gathered all the leaders of the provinces to dedicate the image. He then declared that whoever didn't worship the image would be thrown into a furnace. But the newly appointed officials in Nebuchadnezzar's office refused to worship the golden calf; they were Jewish (Dan. 2:49; 3:13–15). The king was told about the men's refusal to worship the object and, filled with anger, the king sent for them and challenged them.

The men boldly answered:

> "O Nebuchadnezzar, we have no need to answer you in this matter. If this be so, our God whom we serve is able to deliver us from the burning fiery furnace, and he will deliver us out of your hand, O king. But if not, be it known to you, O king, that we will not serve your gods or worship the golden image that you have set up." (Dan. 3:16–18)

What brave men! Under no circumstance would they be willing to worship anything or anyone except for the one true God. They would rather face death than compromise their faith.

The king became furious, and he ordered the furnace to be heated seven times hotter than normal. Bound and fully clothed, the men were tossed into the fire. When the king looked, he noticed that they were unbound and were walking with a fourth person (an angel, or possibly a physical appearance of Christ before the incarnation) who wasn't in the furnace before (Dan. 3:19–27).

Upon realizing the men were not going to die, the king ordered them to leave the furnace. What followed was an interesting edict. The king said,

> "Blessed be the God of Shadrach, Meshach, and Abednego, who has sent his angel and delivered his servants, who trusted in him, and set aside the king's command, and yielded up their bodies rather than serve and worship any god except their own God." (Dan. 3:28)

It appears that Nebuchadnezzar was afraid of the Lord rather than filled with a fear of the Lord. His words never claimed God as *his* God; rather, the focus was on the God of Shadrach, Meshach, and Abednego. But it is a powerful testimony of how the Lord can use our faith in action to reveal Himself to others. Shadrach, Meshach, and Abednego used their words to proclaim the Lord and their actions to proclaim their faith. Nebuchadnezzar could not deny the power and existence of the Lord even if he wasn't willing to submit his own life to Him at that time.

The question we want to ask ourselves is, what are our golden calves? What are the things that keep us from proclaiming the Lord to our neighbors, coworkers, and family? The faith of Shadrach, Meshach, and Abednego inspires us to boldness, knowing that the Lord is with us. We can, with a true heart, proclaim, "If God is for us, who can be against us?" (Rom. 8:31).

REFLECT

1. What is idolatry?

2. Idols made out of gold or wood are much easier to identity than idols of the heart. What are some idols that you could identify common to men and women (e.g., fame, money, success, etc.)? What is one area that you might consider an idol in your heart?

3. Do you struggle with evangelism or sharing about your Christian faith?

4. Is there anyone in your life you've been wanting to share Jesus with, but haven't? What is preventing you? How might you take steps toward sharing?

The Beaten, Persecuted, and Martyred

In Hebrews 11:35–38, the author continued to list characteristics of the faithful, from women receiving their children back from the dead to those being killed for their faith. Unlike our previous list of faithful who triumphed over most obstacles, this list is characterized by pain, suffering, and death. And in the end, we are reminded once again that all of these saints died without receiving what was promised. We, however, have received what was promised, and what is far better than anything we could have ask for or imagined.

READ | **HEBREWS 11:35-38**

RESPOND

These are the core Bible study questions you'll work through this week:

1. This list is less about characteristics and more about the circumstances these faithful saints experienced. List the situations from verses 35–38.

2. Using cross references, who might fit the descriptions? For example, in verse 35, many believe this is in reference to Elijah (1 Kings 17:17–24) and Elisha (2 Kings 4:18–37). Don't be surprised if, when cross referencing, you find a story with only one short text related to it.

3. Find their stories in the Scriptures.

4. Hebrews 11 concludes with a reminder of the beginning of the chapter— the faithful received their commendation (v. 2), but they did not receive what was promised (v. 13). According to the rest of the sentence (v. 40), why did they not receive what was promised?

5. What did God provide that is better?

6. What makes your answer to question 5 better?

7. What might he mean by "apart from us . . . " (v. 40)? Also see Revelation 6:11.

8. How are we made perfect?

9. Where is Jesus in these verses? Where do you see the gospel?

10. What do you learn about God and His character in these verses?

11. How might you apply these verses to your life?

Special note: Often when we think of Hebrews 11, we rightly consider the Old Testament saints and stop there. But in applying the text, we see that there are, for example, modern day prisoners (v. 36) and those whom the world is not worthy of (v. 38). Because of the nature of the topic, we are going to put into action the writer's call to remember those who are in prison (Heb. 13:3). Starting on Day Two, we will learn about a man in prison, a group of modern-day martyrs, and bold Stephen, the first recorded martyr after Jesus' death and resurrection. In the reflection section will be a time of prayer. I will guide us in a short prayer, and you will then be prompted to continue praying.

WEEK SIX | DAY ONE

EXPLORE

Suffering as Christ Suffered

READ | HEBREWS 11:36–40; ISAIAH 52:13–53:12

"For to this you have been called, because Christ also suffered for you, leaving you an example, so that you might follow in his steps" (1 Peter 2:21).

As we've seen throughout this study, religious persecution has been happening since the beginning of time. It shouldn't surprise us, even though it is shocking when we do see it. All suffering is difficult, but it is especially difficult when it is the result of injustice. Thankfully, Jesus doesn't minimize our suffering, but rather He sympathizes with it. He understands. He graciously warned us that it would happen. Most of us will never face death for proclaiming Jesus. We may never experience being beaten. But all of us may face mocking or the slow erosion of our right to worship freely; or we could be shunned from our communities as a result of our Christian faith.

Many of you reading this right now may be facing these things. And it's no wonder that the end of Hebrews 11 turns our attention to those who didn't always triumph in the face of danger but rather perished. They died in faith, but not alone.

Jesus is called a man of sorrows (Isa. 53:3). He understands suffering, beatings, and being mocked and ridiculed. He was abandoned by His friends, then He was beaten and hung on a cross. There isn't anyone who knows sorrows more than our

Savior. When we face persecution of any kind, we have a Person to look to. He graciously warned us that the world would hate His followers just as it hated Him (John 15:18).

He was tempted in every way, but was without sin, so we can run to Him when we are tempted to despair in the face of fear (Heb. 4:14–16). Thank God that we get to go to Him, and that He is the one who is interceding for us. Because we know Jesus, we can endure suffering. We have a Savior who gets it and who is not sitting idle. He is working for us, interceding for us, and carrying our burdens.

Because we know the end of the story, we can read these verses with hope. And although these saints had not seen the object of their hope revealed, they still endured with hope. Their hope and our hope are the same: Jesus.

REFLECT

1. From reading the prophecy of Isaiah in Isaiah 52 and 53, list some of the ways Jesus suffered.

2. None of us will suffer exactly like Jesus; specifically, those of us in Christ will never experience the wrath or feel the weight of the sin of the world. Thank You, Jesus. However, the Word tells us we will suffer like Him. Can you give real-life examples of how Christians throughout the world have suffered in similar ways to what you noted above?

3.   Why do you think the Lord warns us that we also will endure persecution and hatred from the world?

4.   We see at the end of this chapter a clear picture that God rescues some and not others. How do you reconcile God's goodness with the suffering in the world? Does that change when you believe that God is sovereign over all things and rescues some but not others? Why?

WEEK SIX | DAY TWO

EXPLORE

Those Who Are Imprisoned

READ | HEBREWS 11:36; 13:3

In December 2019, China sentenced a prominent pastor to nine years in prison. Pastor Wang Yi led the Early Rain Covenant Church, a Protestant church that met illegally—churches in China must submit to the state to be officially recognized.[27] When Wang refused to register with the state, and therefore be influenced by the state, he and several of his congregants were arrested. Although there may be additional terminology, churches that operate independently of the state are generally called "underground churches." His church was not the only one being seized and shut down by the Chinese government; but due to Wang's prominence and the sheer number of people arrested, the situation made headlines around the world. It is estimated that of the sixty million Christians in China, half are meeting in unregistered churches.[28]

There's a reason we are urged to remember those who are imprisoned (Heb. 13:3). Not much about my day reminds me of the current reality of Christians being persecuted around the world. I'm working, or taking care of my husband and children, or serving my local church. I live in a land of freedom, for now, and have few reminders in my day-to-day to remember those in prison. It takes effort to remember those suffering for their faith under the reign of terror.

---

27. Associated Press, "Outspoken Chinese Pastor Wang Yi Sentenced to 9 Years in Prison," *Christianity Today*, December 30, 2019, https://www.christianitytoday.com/news/2019/december/chinese-pastor-wang-yi-early-rain-house-church-sentence-pri.html.
28. Emily Feng, "China Sentences Christian Leader to 9 Years in Prison," NPR, December 30, 2019, https://www.npr.org/2019/12/30/792293186/china-sentences-christian-leader-to-9-years-prison.

So, today, as we consider those imprisoned for their faith in the past and remember those who are currently in prison for their faith, let's go before the throne of grace on their behalf in prayer.

PRAYER FOR THOSE IN PRISON

Dear Father, we praise Your name and thank You that we can come before You on behalf of those in prison. Lord, we confess that we have not always remembered our brothers and sisters as You've commanded us to. But we are thankful knowing that You never forget them. Lord, would You draw near to those who are brokenhearted and anxiously awaiting rescue? We pray that each Christian would sense Your nearness and would be comforted. Give them faith, more faith than they could imagine, Lord. Give them boldness to stand strong as they lean on You in their weakness. We thank You for Your everlasting love and the promise that nothing can separate them from Your love. Amen.

REFLECT

1. Continue praying for those who are imprisoned.

2. What are ways you can practically remember the persecuted church?

WEEK SIX | DAY THREE

EXPLORE

Those Killed with a Sword

READ | HEBREWS 11:37

On January 8, 1956, a hopeful group of missionaries lost their lives when the people they longed to reach with the gospel attacked and killed them with spears. I'm not sure if there's a more familiar modern story of martyrdom than that of Jim Elliot. Although Elliot's name is the most prominent one, a prominence he would have never sought on his own, he was joined by four others: Ed McCully, Roger Youderian, Pete Fleming, and Nate Saint. The men had traveled into the jungle of Ecuador to reach the Huaorani people. They had been there, giving gifts and getting to know a few of the natives before they were attacked and killed. Their bodies were dumped in a river, and their families were left without their loved ones.

Their stories have been documented in books, articles, movies, and much more. What happened after the murders was nothing less than a miracle. Two of the surviving family members of the victims went back to live with the Huaorani people and share the love of Jesus with them. My eyes well up with tears at the thought of this degree of mercy, forgiveness, and grace. Elisabeth Elliot, widow of Jim Elliot, spent two years in the remote area. Elisabeth, and thousands of missionaries after her, took the words of her late husband to heart: "He is no fool who gives what he cannot keep to gain that which he cannot lose."[29]

The team of men were no fools. They lost their lives, but they could not lose the love of the Lord. They could not lose their life-everlasting, and they could not lose

---

29. Jim Elliot, *The Journals of Jim Elliot*, ed. Elisabeth Elliot (Grand Rapids, MI: Revell, 1978), 174.

the rewards awaiting them. Jesus said: "And do not fear those who kill the body but cannot kill the soul" (Matt. 10:28).

"Blessed are you when people hate you and when they exclude you and revile you and spurn your name as evil, on account of the Son of Man! Rejoice in that day, and leap for joy, for behold, your reward is great in heaven; for so their fathers did to the prophets" (Luke 6:22–23).

Elisabeth Elliot wrote of the aftermath:

> To the world at large this was a sad waste of five young lives. But God has His plan and purpose in all things. There were those whose lives were changed by what happened on Palm Beach. In Brazil, a group of Indians at a mission station deep in the Mato Grosso, upon hearing the news, dropped to their knees and cried out to God for forgiveness for their own lack of concern for fellow Indians who did not know of Jesus Christ. . . . An Air Force Major stationed in England, with many hours of jet flying, immediately began making plans to join the Missionary Aviation Fellowship.[30]

The martyred missionaries join the prophets of old who were ridiculed, reviled, and even killed on account of Jesus. Like those Old Testament saints, we learn about their faith and thank God for their examples. Their reward is great in heaven.

PRAYER FOR MISSIONARIES

Our Father, there are many unreached people groups, and we are thankful that You are patient to return so that many may be reached. I pray that You would raise up men and women willing to go and preach the gospel all over the world. Lord, protect those who are already on the mission field. Give them favor among the people. Prepare the hearts of many to receive Your Word. Provide for those serving who may need medical, material, and psychological help, Lord. Strengthen them, hold them up by Your righteous right hand. Jesus, You are worthy to be praised. We worship You. Amen.

---

30. Elisabeth Elliot, *Through Gates of Splendor* (Carol Stream, IL: Tyndale Momentum, 1956), 247–48.

REFLECT

1.   Continue praying for missionaries.

2.   What are ways that we can be involved in missionary work at home if we are not called to the mission field?

EXPLORE

Of Whom the World Was Not Worthy

READ | HEBREWS 11:38; ACTS 6–7

Stephen is the first recorded martyr after the death of Jesus. The Hellenists (Greek-speaking Jews) were frustrated with the Hebrews for not caring for their widows. Stephen was chosen to serve the widows on behalf of the disciples. He was known as "a man full of faith and of the Holy Spirit" (see Acts 6:1–6).

Stephen was bold and powerful, wise and faithful to preach the good news. He was also despised. Various groups rose up against him and began spreading lies, eventually seizing him as a result of what was said about him. The hatred that Stephen experienced was the same that those before him experienced, Jesus experienced, and exactly what Jesus warned us that we would experience too.

Stephen responded to the charges against him by recounting the Old Testament history—much of the history we've already studied through Hebrews 11. But it's the end of this speech that incensed his listeners. He rebuked Israel for not accepting Jesus as their Messiah and then charged them with killing the prophets (Acts 7:51–53).

Their fury was such that they even ground their teeth (v. 54). And in what appears to be a mob attack, Stephen was stoned. Before his death, he called out to the Lord and asked Him not to hold his attackers' sin against them, similar to Jesus' own desire for God to forgive those who killed Him (Acts 7:60; Luke 23:34). I can't help but think of Elisabeth Elliot as I read about Stephen's heart of forgiveness and mercy. Both Stephen and Elisabeth were clearly gripped by the example of Jesus and the heart of God.

Stephen's murder had a great impact on the church. It may have been one of the catalysts for the apostle Paul's conversion. Paul (also known as Saul) was there cheering on the crowd as Stephen was stoned to death. Later, Paul lamented his actions against the church and Stephen (Acts 22:20).

For many around the world, whether or not to share their faith in Jesus is a life or death decision. But Stephen wasn't an outsider; he was part of the culture the disciples were serving. Stephen was Jewish and more specifically Hellenist yet he had trusted in Jesus (Acts 6:1–6). He could have decided not to share and shrink back in fear or to deny Jesus altogether. Because of his knowledge of the Old Testament, he could easily have been, like Saul, a Pharisee of Pharisees (Phil. 3:5). But he proclaimed the gospel, and he died still proclaiming.

The world was not worthy of Stephen nor any person who has died on account of proclaiming Jesus. One of the most loving things you and I can do as Christians is to share the good news with those around us. The writer of Hebrews emphasized how undeserving sinful man is to hear that news—our sin is why the world is not worthy (Heb. 11:38). None of us are worthy of this gift. But God. He is rich in mercy and continues to allow His mission to forge ahead. And He allows you and me to be participants in His ongoing mission in this world.

PRAYER FOR BOLDNESS TO SHARE

God of mercy, grace, love, and justice, I am in awe of You and Your work around the world. Thank You for Your saving grace in my life—a free gift that I could never have earned. God, I pray You would help me think about those around me who do not know You. You know who they are. Before the foundation of the world, You had them in mind. Would You give me power, like Stephen, through Your Holy Spirit, to share Your gospel? Would You open the hearts of hearers to receive Your saving grace? Lord, thank You for the privilege of doing ministry in this world. Jesus, thank You for Your life, death, and resurrection. Amen.

REFLECT

1. Continue praying for boldness to share and for those who might need to hear.

2. Stephen was not only sharing the gospel; he was rebuking the people who had already denied Jesus. But one thing we see here and throughout the New Testament is the use of Scripture to share or make the point. How might you use the Word of God to share about Jesus with unbelievers?

WEEK SIX | DAY FIVE

Something Better for Us

READ | HEBREWS 11:39-40

You know that question you might use as an icebreaker or maybe in a job interview . . . the "name three people in the past you'd bring to dinner" question? My answer changes depending on the day I'm asked. Recently, my answer was the apostle Paul, Martin Luther King Jr., and Ella Fitzgerald. I'd cook a kickin' meal and ask no less than one thousand questions. But after studying Hebrews 11, I think I'd rotate out dinner with each of the Old Testament saints. My first question would likely be: *How did you endure never seeing the fulfillment of the promise while experiencing some of the most challenging circumstances people could ever face?*

If you have read the devotionals this week, I intentionally drew your attention to modern day saints or those who, at the very least, knew Jesus had lived, died, and is alive. But all of those who came before them only saw a shadow of what the Lord had in store for them. They put their faith in what was promised and received their commendation, but didn't receive that which was promised. They died in faith (Heb. 11:2, 13). The Lord was waiting to provide something far better for all of us: Jesus.

The old covenant has passed away—Jesus provided the way for the new covenant to be established:

Now the point in what we are saying is this: we have such a high priest, one who is seated at the right hand of the throne of the Majesty in heaven, a minister in the holy places, in the true tent that the Lord set up, not man. For every high priest is appointed to offer gifts and sacrifices; thus it is necessary for this priest also to have something to offer. Now if he were on earth, he would not be a priest at all, since there are priests who offer gifts according to the law. They serve a copy and shadow of the heavenly things. For when Moses was about to erect the tent, he was instructed by God, saying, "See that you make everything according to the pattern that was shown you on the mountain." But as it is, Christ has obtained a ministry that is as much more excellent than the old as the covenant he mediates is better, since it is enacted on better promises. For if that first covenant had been faultless, there would have been no occasion to look for a second. (Heb. 8:1–7)

We could easily spend six weeks just unpacking those verses.

It's such good news.

It doesn't mean that we can now do whatever we desire. We are still called to be holy as God is holy (1 Peter 1:16–17). And it doesn't mean that the Old Testament (or more specifically the law of Moses) is not important—truly to understand the Lord at all we must grow in understanding the law of the Lord (Ps. 1:2; 119:1). All Scripture is profitable (2 Tim. 3:16–17). The good news is Jesus fulfilled the law—we no longer must sacrifice a lamb. He ushered in the better, superior, eternal covenant with all the benefits accounted to Him now accounted to us!

The Old Testament saints died waiting for Jesus. But they believed and trusted the Savior. They had faith that God would do what He said He would do. We are waiting. We are waiting for Jesus to return. We are enduring pain, sorrows, and death. And the Lord graciously gave us these examples so we might endure with hope.

PRAY FOR FAITH

Lord, thank You for fulfilling all of Your promises and for the promises yet to be fulfilled. I confess to not always believing You, Lord. I join my brother and say "I believe, help my unbelief." You are kind to us to reveal the stories of men and women who had faith to believe and died in that faith. Thank You for sustaining them, Lord. I pray You would increase my faith as I wait for Jesus to return and make all things new. Hold me fast, Lord; keep me close to You. You are my rock and salvation, my redeemer. Amen.

REFLECT

1. Continue to pray for faith for specific areas of your life where faith and trust are lacking.

2. List all the ways that Jesus is better. What are the benefits of being found in Jesus and rewards that we receive?

CONCLUSION

The Founder and Perfecter of Our Faith

READD | **HEBREWS 12:1–2**

Note: If you are doing the eight-week option, this conclusion will be your core study and reflection questions for the week. You will end here. If you are doing the six-week option, then read through this section as the conclusion to the study.

If we want to apply all that we've learned in Hebrews 11, Hebrews 12:1–2 is a good, if not necessary, place to start. It's here we understand the context of our faith and how to walk out our faith. It's here that we also get a beautiful picture of how the Old Testament saints and all those who've gone before us function now.

> Therefore, since we are surrounded by so great a cloud of witnesses, let us also lay aside every weight, and sin which clings so closely, and let us run with endurance the race that is set before us, looking to Jesus, the founder and perfecter of our faith, who for the joy that was set before him endured the cross, despising the shame, and is seated at the right hand of the throne of God. (Heb. 12:1–2)

Have you ever watched the 100-meter hurdles? Runners line up, as if running a 100-meter dash, but every ten meters or so there is a structure that the sprinters must jump over. I know this particular sporting event well because I used to compete in it. I loved it. I was agile and flexible—able to glide over the hurdles well. But every now and then, I'd hit a hurdle with one of my legs, messing up my rhythm and sometimes tumbling to the ground. I'd get myself together and finish the race. I never quit, no matter how tough it got.

When I think about the Christian walk of faith, it feels like a hurdle event. You start sprinting and running hard and then you have to jump over some obstacle. You find your rhythm and jump again and then again . . . over and over again, stumbling at times, but never stopping. You and I run that same race. And according to Hebrews 12:1, we don't run it alone.

The readers of this letter would have related to this idea of the hurdles. They were exhorted not to forget how they endured hard times but persevered (Heb. 11:32–39). The cloud of witnesses would have also understood enduring through various trials, for each one of them had to fight the good fight of faith. So, we are not alone because all of those who have gone before us have experienced walking by faith and not by sight (2 Cor. 5:7).

Those before us witnessed to the goodness and faithfulness of God. There's something comforting about knowing that men and women have finished their races well for centuries—it gives me faith that I can too.

The writer of Hebrews wants to also draw our attention to part of what it takes to run the race of faith. When I ran the hurdles, I wore lightweight clothes. When you go on a run, if you add layers upon layers of clothes, you quickly become encumbered by the weight of it all. It would be impossible to sprint well in heavy gear—you might still run, but you'd run slowly. You wouldn't jump over the hurdles; you'd likely crash right into them.

You and I struggle with something that's like those extra garments that make running tough. Sin ("weight" or "impediment") is like the heavy garments that weigh us down and make it difficult to run. Like those who have gone before us, we are exhorted to lay that weight—our sin—aside. A recognition of our struggles with sin is not meant to burden us or condemn us. Just the opposite! As we recognize our struggles, we can then receive grace. If we confess our sin, God is faithful to forgive us and to purify us (1 John 1:9). There's no longer any condemnation for us (Rom. 8:1). And when we set our eyes on Jesus and what He has done, then we can run the race well.

When you are running a race, whether it's the sprint that I've been referring to or any road race, the proper form is for your head to be up and your gaze to be straight in front of you. Where you set your eyes matters. No surprise to me that the writer in Hebrews encourages us to do likewise. It's interesting, however, that the author doesn't tell us to fix our eyes on the finish line—at least not in these verses and in the context of running the race with faith. We aren't looking at the future; we are looking at Jesus who secures our future.

Right now, you and I have the privilege of knowing the promise the people of old never saw fulfilled while on earth. The author and perfecter of our faith: Jesus. We can run this race set before us because He ran His race with joy, endured the cross, despised the shame, and is right now seated at the right hand of God (Heb. 12:2). You and I look to Jesus who lived a perfect life, endured a shameful death, absorbed the wrath of God, defeated death, and lives to make intercession for us (Heb. 7:25).

Although we thank God for all of those who have gone before us, they are not where we put our faith and where we fix our eyes. We can emulate their faith, but let's fix our eyes on Jesus.

REFLECT

1.   Some would say that the cloud of witnesses is surrounding us and watching us—cheering us on. It reminds me of my track running days and those in the stands cheering me on to the finish line. Others would say it is a metaphor and that the cloud of witnesses are meant to be witnessing to us by their example. However you interpret the text, how might it encourage you that there is a "cloud of witnesses"?

2.   Why do you think that the writer emphasizes putting off sin and all things that hinder us to run the race set before us? What are practical ways you can lay aside these weights?

3.   How might you fight the temptation to legalism—trying to earn favor before the Lord—in this race set before you since you know you are saved by grace?

4.   Where is Jesus in these verses? Where do you see the gospel?

5.   What do you learn about God and His character in these verses?

6.   How might you apply these verses to your life?

If we've learned anything through studying the lives of those who have gone before us, it's that this walk of faith can be difficult. Like the great cloud of witnesses, you and I will endure trials of many kinds throughout our lives too. And we aren't called to do it on our own. As the writer of Hebrews exhorted us in Hebrews 10: "And let us consider how to stir up one another to love and good works, not neglecting to meet together, as is the habit of some, but encouraging one another, and all the more as you see the Day drawing near" (vv. 24–25). You and I need others to encourage us to keep running.

Some of you have been hurt by others, and it can be tempting to withdraw from community as a result. As we have seen, we serve a God who is not far off. Ask your heavenly Father for help in finding a local church and community within the church where you can be served and serve others. Others of you long for community. You too have a God who is near. Ask Him for friends. He cares about our every need.

Wherever you are in your faith, don't go it alone. Let's pursue community as we fix our eyes on Jesus for the race set before us.

RESOURCES FOR FURTHER STUDY

You and I will get to learn about the Lord for all eternity. I imagine asking Him many questions like, "How exactly does the Trinity work?" We are all students, learning what we can as we read and as the Lord illuminates His Word to us. I find the whole mystery and lack of knowledge to be delightful. I will never exhaust learning about Him. The opportunity is limitless. Thankfully, there are a number of people who make it their aim to learn Greek and Hebrew and go to the original text in an attempt to interpret it for the benefit of all of us! If you find yourself, like me, hungry to know even more about the context of Hebrews, the meaning of words, and the possible intent of the author, you'll want to grab these additional resources.

F. F. Bruce, *The Epistle to the Hebrews*, Grand Rapids, MI: William B. Eerdmans Publishing Company, 1990.

Philip Edgcumbe Hughes, *A Commentary on the Epistle to the Hebrews*, Grand Rapids, MI: William B. Eerdmans Publishing Company, 1977.

Tremper Longman III and David E. Garland, *The Expositor's Bible Commentary, Hebrews—Revelation*, Grand Rapids, MI: Zondervan, 2006.

Thomas R. Schreiner, *Biblical Theology for Christian Proclamation: Commentary on Hebrews*, Nashville, TN: Holman Reference, 2015.

Jen Wilkin, *Better: A Study of Hebrews*, Nashville, TN: LifeWay Press, 2019.

APPENDIX A

A NOTE TO BIBLE STUDY LEADERS

I'm so grateful that you would choose *A Great Cloud of Witnesses* for your group Bible study. Following are some tips and suggestions using the "What This Study Offers" guide from the beginning of the book. My hope is that these additional notes will assist you in leading an effective Bible study. Whatever you do, your first step should be to look through the study to get a feel for the layout. After you've done that, come back here to read the rest of my brief note to you.

There are several options for how you can lead your group. Are you teaching the text and then doing discussion questions? Will you sit in a circle and go through the questions together without a teaching time at the beginning? How you format the study to fit your group dynamics is the first decision you will need to make. Most Bible studies seem to be in the context of small group. Therefore, the tips below assume that you will be teaching and leading discussion as you sit with participants in a small group context.

WHAT THIS STUDY OFFERS

If you have used my study on Romans 8, *If God Is for Us*, you will be happy to know that the format is quite similar. The biggest difference is that we will spend much of our time in the Old Testament to learn about the life and stories of the members of the Hall of Faith featured in Hebrews 11. This study is not meant to spoon-feed you the answers, although I do try to guide you toward them. The goal is that you will dig into the text and let the questions be your guide.

Extra note for leading: Prepare your group ahead of time by encouraging them to secure this resource at least two weeks ahead of your start date so they can read the

About this Book and Introduction. Or, if you plan to provide the resource on the first day of the study, instruct your group to read the entire book of Hebrews in order to familiarize themselves with the text.

This six-week study is unique in that it is a hybrid—a Bible study and devotional. Each week will include the following:

- A brief introduction to the week's study.

- Weekly "Read" prompts to get you into the Word.

- "Respond" questions to help you dig into what you've read and understand it better. These are the core Bible study questions you'll work through each week.

- Five days' worth of "Explore" devotionals each week to support you in thinking about the text and applying it to your life.

- Five days' worth of "Reflect" questions to give you more to think and pray about.

Extra note for leading: Prepare to discuss and work through the core Bible study questions found at the beginning of each week under "Explore." They provide a general overview of the text, and the line-by-line questions help guide participants through studying God's Word. The goal of the Bible study is for participants to be able to read the Bible for themselves; therefore, the questions are meant to direct each person to answers that explain the context, meaning, and application.

Consider preparing the answers ahead of time. When you teach, you could then ask the questions one by one. Or you could teach an overview of the text at the beginning of each group study session.

This study is also unique because of who I've chosen to focus our attention on. We will not study every Old Testament person named in Hebrews 11. I have decided to give greater attention to little-known or studied people such as Enoch, Rahab, and Gideon. Toward the end of the study we will also look at a few modern-day martyrs and spend time in prayer.

Extra note for leading: The devotionals allow for greater focus on the individual characters and, as already mentioned, we are not focusing on well-known and often studied characters, such as David. You may choose to use one of the devotionals as your guide for discussion. If you choose to use a devotional for the discussion, you might suggest that each participant do the core Bible study questions ("Explore") on their own. Another option would be to teach using the "Explore" questions, and then use one of the devotionals or a combination of the devotional questions as part of the discussion.

If you decide to teach the text and use a devotional as your guide, I highly recommend asking the three questions at the end of each core Bible study section:

1.   Where is Jesus in these verses? Where do you see the gospel?

2.   What do you learn about God and His character in these verses?

3.   How might you apply these verses to your life?

These three questions are *not* asked in the devotional questions labeled "Reflect." The devotional questions are geared toward reflection and application. However, if you do not use the core Bible study questions as a guide for discussion, adding these questions will help keep your discussion centered on the gospel and God as the subject of the text.

MAKE IT WORK FOR YOU!

I encourage you to take advantage of the flexibility built into this study to make it work for you. It's designed to be done in a group setting or individually. Here are a few of the possibilities.

- Do the study entirely on your own at home.

- Meet daily with a few friends in person (maybe for coffee) or online to share your response to the devotionals and the questions.

- Gather with a larger group through Bible studies offered at your church.

- Try a combination—do some of it (like the devotionals) at home and some of it (like selected study or reflection questions) in a weekly group gathering. Or study at home and then come together to discuss your insights and discoveries.

You can follow the suggested pattern of five days of study, two days off, or you can stretch out the material to cover six or even seven days. Personally, I like the idea of reading and study on one day, devotionals and reflections on five more days, and then taking a "sabbath" day of rest.

Extra note for leading: Because this study is geared for both home study and group study, I would suggest that you make it clear to your participants the option you are going to do so they come prepared and ready to study. I would also suggest that the participants read one day ahead of the study. For example, for the first week you might suggest that they come having already read Hebrews 10 (and hopefully the entire book but especially Hebrews 10). Depending on the size of the group, you might also decide to read it aloud together.

SIX OR EIGHT WEEK OPTIONS

This study also provides the flexibility to complete it in six or eight weeks! Within the study are two natural breaks that allow for extending the timeline to eight weeks. The first is in "Week One: Assurance of Things Hoped For." In the Respond section, simply stop at question 7, then begin week two with question 8. The second place is the conclusion at the end of the study. The conclusion, focused on Hebrews 12:1–3, is meant to be read as a devotional and applied, but can also stand alone as the study for week eight.

SIX WEEKS

Week One: Once for All

Week Two: The Possibility of Faith

Week Three: The Well-Known

Week Four: A Faith That Points to Jesus

Week Five: The Powerful and Faithful

Week Six: The Beaten, Persecuted, and Martyred

Conclusion: The Founder and Perfecter of Our Faith

EIGHT WEEKS

Week One: Once for All (ending with Respond question #7)

Week Two: Once for All continued (beginning with Respond question #8)

Week Three: The Possibility of Faith

Week Four: The Well-Known

Week Five: A Faith That Points to Jesus

Week Six: The Powerful and Faithful

Week Seven: The Beaten, Persecuted, and Martyred

Week Eight (Conclusion): The Founder and Perfecter of Our Faith

I hope this short note helps you as you lead your group into the glorious reality that Jesus is better!

APPENDIX B

FOUR PRACTICAL GUIDELINES FOR READING OLD TESTAMENT STORIES

Hebrews 11 took us on a tour of some of the most iconic stories in the Old Testament. But those stories aren't meant to be read in a vacuum. For the purpose of Hebrews 11, they are meant to point us toward greater faith and faithfulness. But if you and I want to better understand the Bible—how to read it, and how and when to apply it—we will want to read each story in its full context or even read the entire book each stems from. So, I've asked an Old Testament scholar to help us learn how to read the stories of old and apply them to our lives. My hope is that as you finish up this study, you'll be hungry to study Genesis, Exodus, Joshua, Judges, and all the other books that were highlighted throughout our time together.

FOUR PRACTICAL GUIDELINES FOR READING
OLD TESTAMENT STORIES

Dr. George H. Guthrie

Harold Goddard writes, "The [destiny] of the world is determined less by the battles that are lost and won than by the stories it loves and believes in."[31] As we live in the modern world, we see the evidence of Goddard's statement all around us. People have particular views of the world, and those views often are driven by the stories they have embraced.

God wants to pull us into His Story and shape us by it. You may not be terribly familiar with the Old Testament stories, which play a vitally important role in tell-

---

31. "The destiny of the world is determined less by the battles that are lost and won than by the stories it loves and believes in" is a quote from Harold Goddard's *The Meaning of Shakespeare*, vol. 2 (Chicago: The University of Chicago Press, 1951), 208.

ing the Grand Story, but there are a number of reasons why you should read those stories (which make up a bit less than 50 percent of the Old Testament). You really can't make sense of the New Testament unless you "get" the Old Testament (see Heb. 1:1–2a). The Old Testament narrative material is *great* literature, and the people, events, power struggles, personal crises, and hope we find in these stories often are as relevant as this morning's news. Thus, the Old Testament stories, read in the right way, form an indispensable resource for Christian living.

But if you are like most of us, you need a bit of help in *how* to engage those stories really well. Here are four beginning thoughts.

1. Read the story in light of the bigger STORY of which it is a part!

Most of the Old Testament stories have a broader literary context—and a broader historical context—that can help us understand the dynamics we see in a given story. For example, when we read the story of Jacob, Esau, and "the stolen blessing" of Genesis 27, it may be a bit hard to understand why Rebekah, Jacob and Esau's mom, instructed Jacob to deceive Isaac, taking the blessing that by order of birth should have gone to his slightly older brother. From the story it is clear that a) Rebekah was partial to Jacob, who was a momma's boy (Gen. 25:28), so that is one reason she acted as she did, and b) this family had some dysfunction going! But was there something else behind Rebekah's action? In Gen 25:21–24 we read an important bit of context:

"Isaac prayed to the LORD on behalf of his wife because she was childless. The LORD heard his prayer, and his wife Rebekah conceived. But the children inside her struggled with each other, and she said, 'Why is this happening to me?' So she went to inquire of the LORD. And the LORD said to her:

> *Two nations are in your womb;*
> *two people will come from you and be separated.*
> *One people will be stronger than the other,*
> *and the older will serve the younger.*

When her time came to give birth, there were indeed twins in her womb."
(Gen. 25:21–24 HCSB)

Notice the prophecy Rebekah received: "The older will serve the younger." It may be, therefore, that Rebekah was motivated to help Jacob get the blessing from Isaac because she felt that his superiority over Esau was ordained by God. This doesn't excuse the deception involved (that trait is woven through this family), but it may help explain it.

2. Read the story in light of its purpose.

Sometimes there are clues in the story or its broader context that tell us something about what the author wants us to learn from the story. For instance, have you ever been put off by the story of Jephthah in Judges 11:29–40? I have. In that story Jephthah makes a very stupid vow, saying to the Lord, "If You will hand over the Ammonites to me, whatever comes out of the doors of my house to greet me when I return in peace from the Ammonites will belong to the LORD, and I will offer it as a burnt offering" (11:30–31 HCSB). While animals at times were kept in a stall area of a house, his family also lived there, of course. So when Jephthah had come home from his victory, his daughter came out to meet him. He was devastated and said, "I have given my word to the LORD and cannot take it back" (11:35 HCSB). She got burned—literally. Horrible story! It is *meant* to be horrible to make a point. Do you know the purpose? It is one of many stories in Judges that demonstrate, "This is the kind of stupidity that happens when you forget God's law!" You see, if Jephthah had known the law of God, he would have known the part that said:

"Or if someone swears rashly to do what is good or evil—concerning anything a person may speak rashly in an oath—without being aware of it, but later recognizes it, he incurs guilt in such an instance." (Lev. 5:4 HCSB)

The passage goes on to tell how such a guilty person can be forgiven by making a restitution offering. The sin is atoned for. You see, Jephthah did not have to keep his vow to offer his daughter as a burnt offering. He could have offered a female lamb instead and could have been forgiven for his sin of making a rash vow. Judges uses Jephthah, in other words, as a bad example, an example of a person who does not know God's word!

3. Understand important cultural elements in the story.

When we understand more about the culture surrounding a biblical story, it can help us get the full effect of the story. These often can make a story more meaningful or the impact more powerful. For instance, think about the story of David and Goliath in 1 Samuel 17. Now when we think of a "slingshot," we think of a children's toy. But did you know that slings were used as serious weapons in the Ancient Near East? In Israel shepherds used slings to fight off wild animals, but they also could be used in battle, as reflected in this striking story (pardon the pun). Sling stones could be 3+ inches in diameter (the size of a peach!), could be slung *hundreds* of feet, and could travel over 100 miles per hour! Can you imagine what such a rock would do if it hit you in the head?! David did not strike Goliath down with a toy. Rather, he was skilled with a weapon that gave him a strategic advantage! He could kill the big brute without ever getting near him! That type of information can bring a story to life.

4. Read the story, recognizing God as the Hero.

For instance, the David and Goliath story of 1 Samuel 17 often is presented with David as the paradigmatic hero. But notice what we read on the lips of David himself:

"The LORD . . . will rescue me from the hand of this Philistine." (17:37 HCSB)

"I come against you in the name of Yahweh of Hosts, the God of Israel's armies—you have defied Him." (17:45 HCSB)

"Today, the LORD will hand you over to me." (17:46 HCSB)

"The battle is the LORD's. He will hand you over to us." (17:47 HCSB)

In the Old Testament stories, God is the ultimate hero, not any human being. God is the one working out the salvation of His people. Seeing Him as the ultimate hero gives us an important frame of reference for reading the Old Testament stories.[32]

---

32. Dr. George Guthrie is an Old Testament scholar and agreed to share his insights. You can find his work featured at https://georgehguthrie.com. This article was adapted from "4 Practical Guidelines for Reading Old Testament Stories," GeorgeHGuthrie.com, September 8, 2016, https://georgehguthrie.com/new-blog/2016/6/10/4-guidelines-for-reading-old-testament-stories.

What would change if you really understood all that God has done and is doing for you?

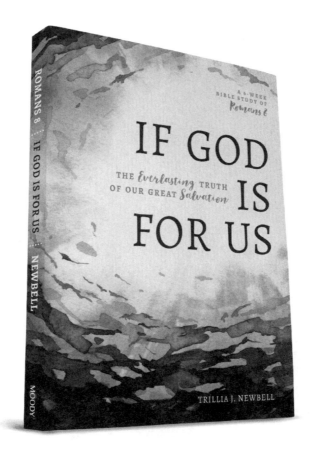

In this 6-week study, Trillia Newbell will walk you through Romans 8 and help you internalize the scandalous truths of our great salvation, our inheritance, the assurance of our faith, and ultimately the love of our good Father.

Each week includes:
- 5 daily readings out of Romans
- A devotional for each daily reading
- Questions for reflection and study

If you've experienced the comfort of Romans 8 before, but want to plant it more deeply in your heart, this is the Bible study for you. And it's great for individual or group settings.

978-0-8024-1713-8 | also available as an eBook

Explore our Bible studies at
moodypublisherswomen.com

MOODY PUBLISHERS
WOMEN
BIBLE STUDIES

More from Trillia Newbell

United will inspire, challenge, and encourage readers to pursue the joys of diversity through stories of the author's own journey and a theology of diversity lived out. In the pages of *United*, Trillia Newbell reveals the deeply moving, transforming power of knowing—*really knowing*—someone who is equal yet unique.

978-0-8024-1014-6

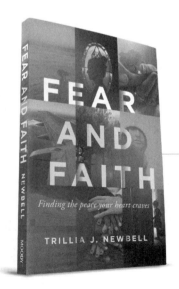

The fears we carry can paralyze our spirit, damage our relationships, and hinder our faith. *Fear and Faith* is a meditation upon God's trustworthiness. By sharing reflections on Scripture, her own experiences, and the stories of other women, Trillia Newbell shows you a God big enough to replace your fears with faith.

978-0-8024-1022-1

Also available as eBooks

MOODY
Publishers®

From the Word **to Life**®

God could have made us all exactly the same, but He didn't. And our differences are good!